A Brief History of Absinthe

Medicine, Art, Poetry, and Ritual

Matthew Leigh Embleton

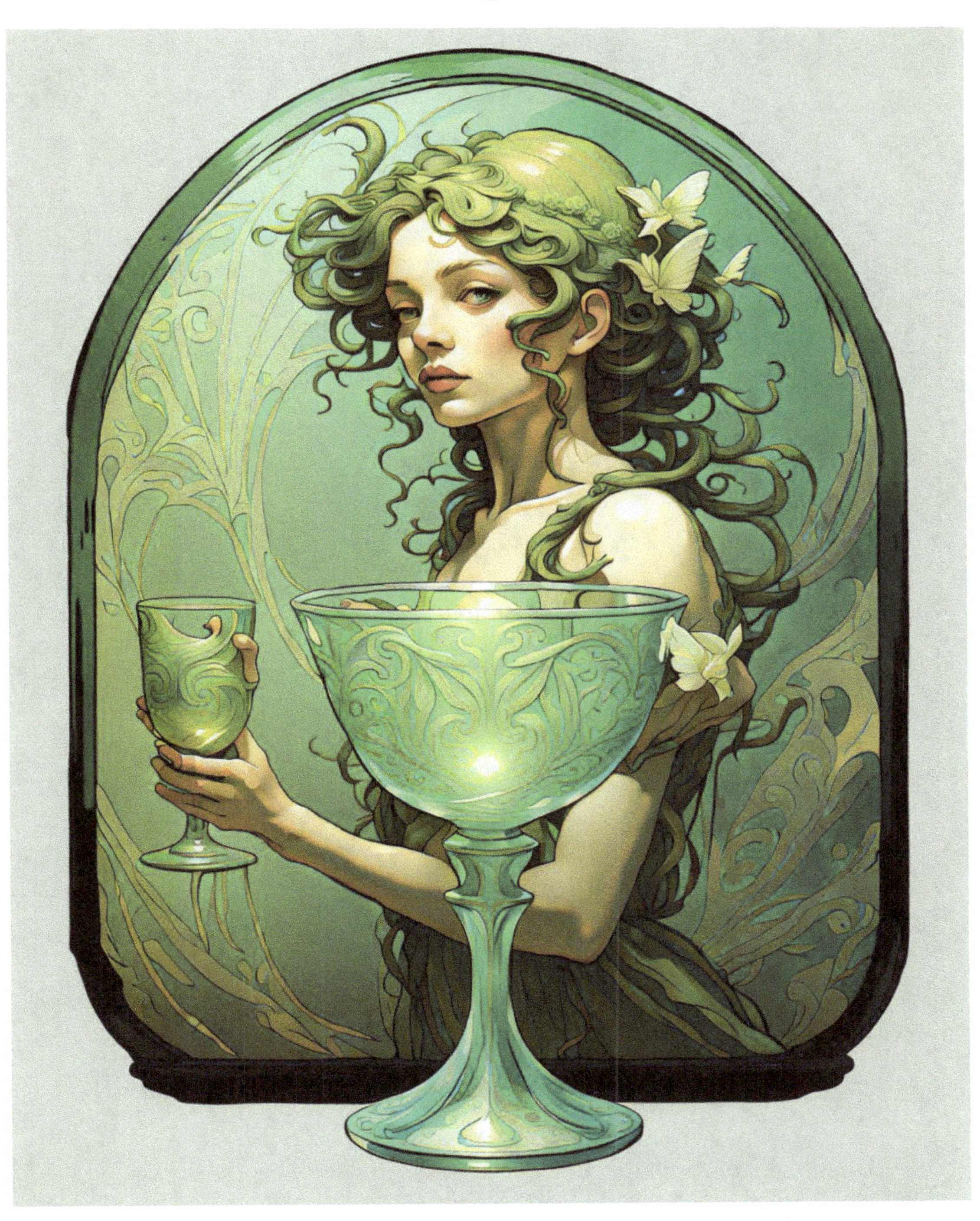

A Brief History of Absinthe

Cover: The Green Fairy, AI generated by the author.

All other images in this book are under the Creative Commons License and are in the Public Domain unless otherwise specified.

Acknowledgments

I have long been fascinated by history, and I am very grateful to the special people in my life who have supported and encouraged me in my work. Thank you for believing in me. You know who you are.

1.   Introduction: Myth and Notoriety

In the summer of 1999 I performed my first gig as an electronic musician at the Global Café in Golden Square, London. Also present that evening was a television crew filming a piece for The London Programme about the reintroduction of absinthe to London's nightlife. (Sadly none of our performance made the final cut, but I could be seen briefly at the bar behind an interviewee for about 7 seconds).

As we performed, the flaming ritual of pouring absinthe over a sugar cube and setting it alight was a crowd pleasing spectacle. The crew interviewed members of the public about their experience, which many described as a kind of clear-headed inebriation, a lucid drunkenness, a mind opening experience. I said to myself that one day I would try it, and then I forgot all about it.

One evening 15 years later, having filled my imagination with the music and art of *La Belle Époque*, I took a walk through Soho and purchased my first bottle of absinthe. At home I dimmed the lights and put on the complete piano works of Debussy softly in the background. Having prepared a glass with the spoon and a sugar cube, I sipped and relaxed, imagining myself at a café somewhere in Paris in the 1880s. It was indeed a mind opening experience. As my mind wandered, ideas and solutions to my problems and frustrations presented themselves to me in moments of clarity.

When discussing this experience with others, the mere mention of the word absinthe made some of them react with a shudder of disapproval, as if I had mentioned something so sordid, shameful, and nefarious, that it was not fit for polite conversation, saying things like:

> *"absinthe is dangerous"... "absinthe is hallucinogenic"*
> *"absinthe is toxic"... "absinthe drives people mad"*
> *"absinthe makes people go blind"... "absinthe made Van Gogh cut his ear off"**
> *"absinthe is for awful people that want to get blind drunk"*
> *"It tastes awful (drinking shots)"*
> *"I know someone who got really drunk on it a few years ago (drinking shots)"*
> *"I got really drunk on it a few years ago (drinking shots)"*
> *"why can't you just have a beer like normal people?"*

…I wondered why this was, why there was so much misinformation on the subject, so many twisted myths, and so much misadventure and mishap in these anecdotes.

The chemical compound thujone, found naturally in absinthe's main ingredient wormwood, appears in such small quantities in absinthe that if you attempted to drink enough of it in order to be psychoactively affected by the thujone, alcohol poisoning would kill you long before the traces of thujone caused you any harm.

Absinthe is not hallucinogenic. The herbal compounds produce some stimulant and some sedative effects which complement each other. If you're lucky, you may have some strange dreams, but whether or not that's because of the absinthe, or facilitated by an enhanced connection with your subconscious mind, is undecided. My research on this question is ongoing.

Absinthe is traditionally drunk diluted with water at a ratio of 3 to 5 parts water to 1 part absinthe. The dilution with the ice cold water unlocks the delicious and complex herbal flavours, and the sugar is used to taste to offset the bitterness of some of those herbal flavours.

Why would anyone drink absinthe as a shot? Perhaps they are drawn to the high alcohol content, maybe as a dare, caught in the moment when drinking shots seems like a good idea. Sadly they are missing out on something much more subtle and refined.

2.   The Magic Ingredients

Wormwood (*Artemisia absinthium*)

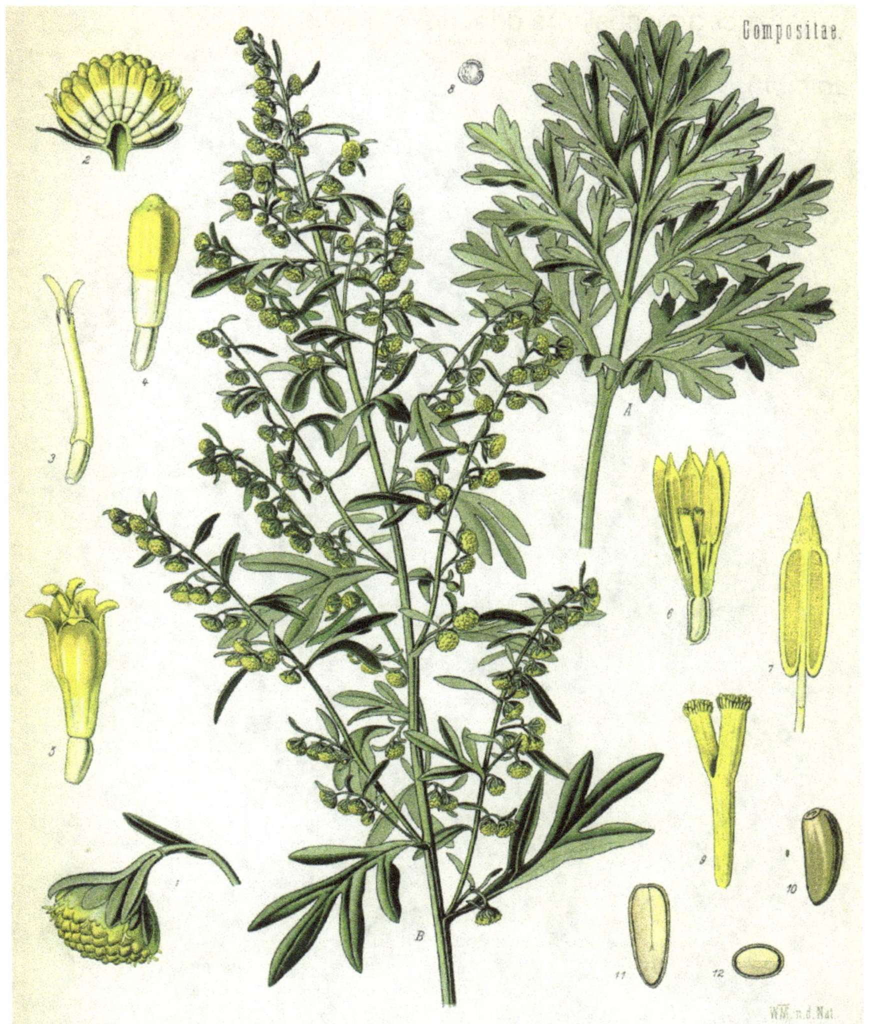

Artemisia Absinthium in Franz Eugen Köhler's *Medizinal-Pflanzen*, 1897

One of the 'Holy Trinity', Wormwood is an alteration of the obscure Old English *wermod*. The German equivalent *wermut* is the source of the term vermouth, used in French and English to describe aromatised fortified wine traditionally flavoured with wormwood.

Its close relative *Artemisia pontica*, known as little absinthe or petite wormwood, is also used to produce absinthe's distinctive green colour.

Artemisia is named after the Greek goddess Artemis, a goddess of childbirth, due to its traditional use as a remedy for complaints affecting the female reproductive organs. Absinthium derives from the Greek term for wormwood, *apsínthion*.

Thujone

Thujone is a chemical compound found naturally in Wormwood in very small trace amounts. It can have mood elevating and stimulating effects in small doses, but the amount of Thujone found in absinthe is so small that it is unlikely to be responsible for much if any of the mood elevating or stimulating effects experienced by absinthe drinkers.

Anise (*Pimpinella anisum*)

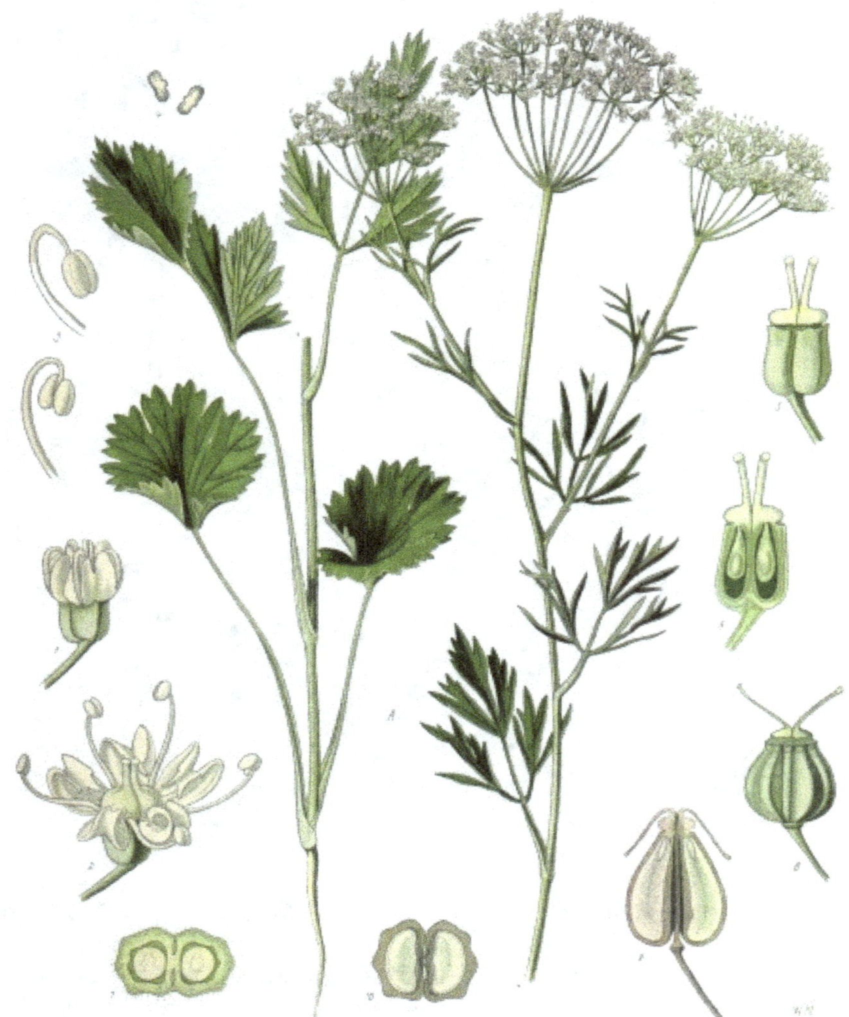

Pimpinella Anisum in Franz Eugen Köhler's *Medizinal-Pflanzen*, 1897

One of the 'Holy Trinity', anise or aniseed has a unique flavour and aroma which is the basis for a number of spirits and liqueurs, particularly around the Mediterranean, including Anis, Anisette, Arak, Galliano, Ouzo, Pastis, Raki, and Sambuca. The name anise is derived via Old French from the Latin words *anīsum* or *anēthum* from the Greek ἄνηθον *ánēthon* referring to dill.

Fennel (*Foeniculum vulgare*)

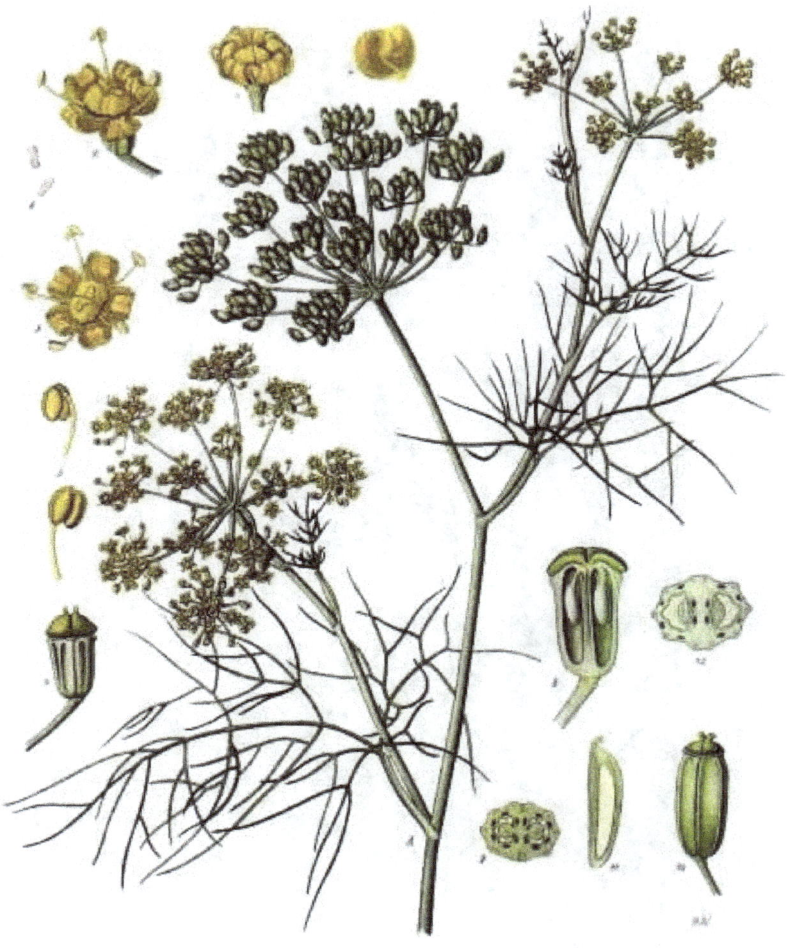

Foeniculum Vulgare in Franz Eugen Köhler's *Medizinal-Pflanzen*, 1897

One of the 'Holy Trinity', fennel is native to the shores of the Mediterranean and it was prized by the Romans and the ancient Greeks as a medicine, food, and insect repellent. In Latin it was known as *faeniculum*, a diminutive of *faenum* meaning hay. In Old French this became *fenoil*, and fennel in Old English.

Florence fennel or finocchio is a variety that has a swollen bulb-like stem that is used as a vegetable. Its flavour is similar to anise and it is used as a herb in cooking.

The aromatic character of fennel comes from volatile oils which give off mixed aromas. Chemical compounds include *trans-anethole* (anise, aniseed), *estragole* (liquorice), *fenchone* (mint), *limonene* (citrus), and *camphor* (insect repelling properties).

Phytochemicals are chemical compounds produced by plants to resist bacteria, which is why they have medicinal properties in treating fungal, bacterial, and viral infections. Phytochemicals found in fennel include *rosmarinic acid* (rosemary), and *luteolin* which is aromatic and used as a yellow dye.

Hyssop (*Hyssopus officinalis*)

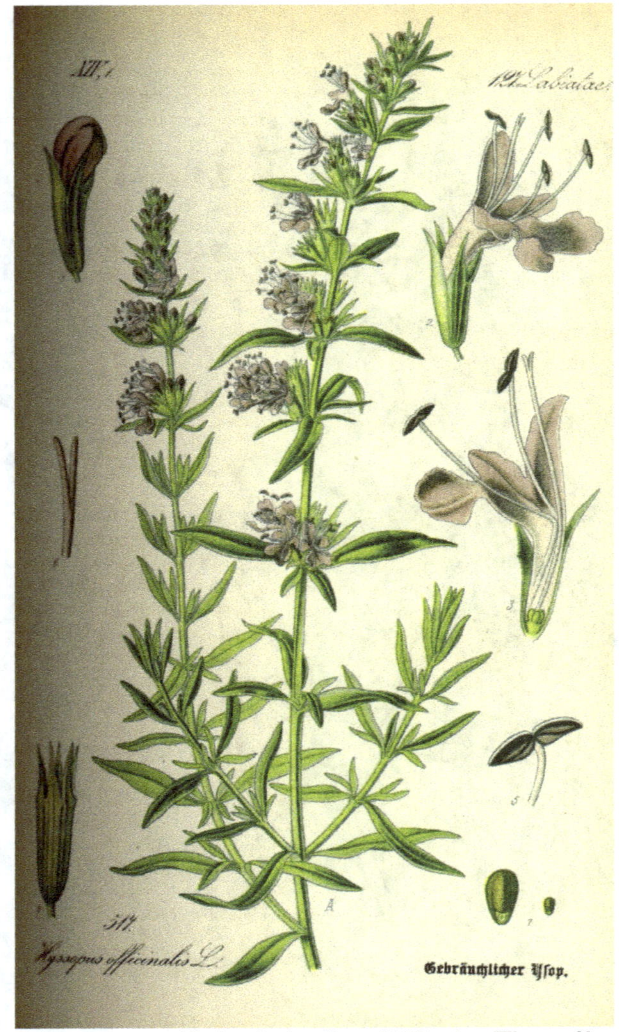

Hyssopus officinalis in Otto Wilhelm Thomé's
Flora von Deutschland, Österreich und der Schweiz, 1885

Hyssop is a key ingredient of absinthe as a main source of its distinctive green colour. It has a slightly bitter taste and a minty aroma, and is also used to make the French herbal liqueur Chartreuse.

Hyssop leaves are used as an aromatic condiment. *Za'atar* is a famous Middle Eastern herbal mixture, some versions of which include dried hyssop leaves.

In herbal medicine hyssop is believed to have soothing, expectorant, and cough suppressant properties. It has been used for centuries in traditional medicine in order to increase circulation and to treat multiple conditions such as coughing and sore throat.

It is also believed that hyssop can stimulate the gastrointestinal system to treat digestion and stomach complaints.

Lemon Balm (*Melissa officinalis*)

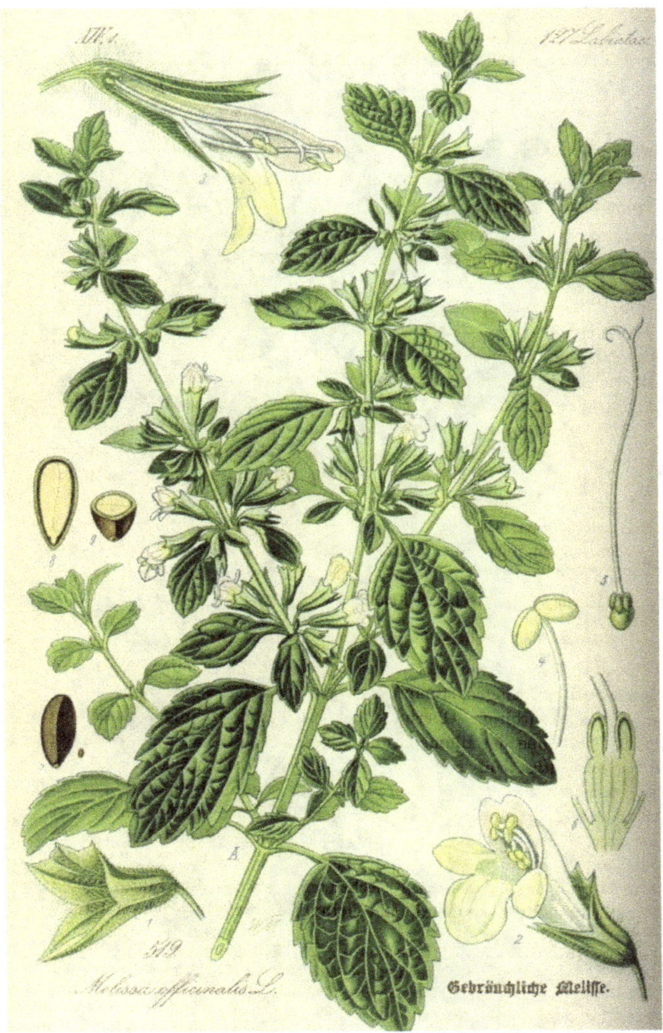

Melissa officinalis in Otto Wilhelm Thomé's
Flora von Deutschland, Österreich und der Schweiz, 1885

Lemon Balm is a member of the mint family and has a mild lemon scent from its leaves. It also has small white flowers of nectar which attract bees, which has led to its use attracting bees for honey production. The name Melissa in Greek means honey bee.

The leaves appear in some herbal teas to aid digestion, and as a flavouring. Its oil is used in perfumery. Its use can be dated to over 2000 years ago by the Romans and the Greeks. It is mentioned in *Historia Plantarum* by Theophrastus as melissófyllon (μελισσόφυλλον) literally 'bee-leaf'.

The English botanist Nicholas Culpeper considered lemon balm to be ruled by the planet Jupiter in Cancer, and suggested it to be used for "weak stomachs", to cause the heart to become "merry", to help digestion, to open "obstructions of the brain", and to expel "melancholy vapours" from the heart and arteries.

Star Anise (*Illicium verum*)

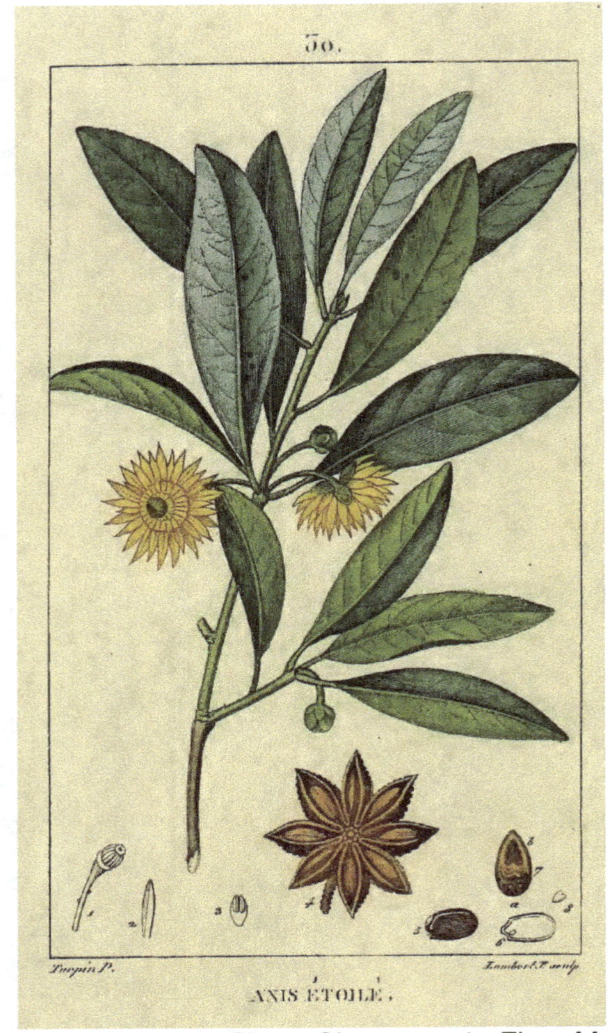

Illicium verum from François-Pierre Chaumeton's *Flore Medicale*, 1833

Star Anise is native to northeast Vietnam and South China, and as a spice it closely resembles the flavour of anise because it contains the same chemical compound anethole. Its oil is a highly fragrant oil used in cooking, perfumery, soaps, toothpastes, mouthwashes, and skin creams. It is a less expensive substitute for anise in baking and liqueur production, as in the liqueur Galliano. Illicum comes from the Latin *illico* meaning entice or seduce. *Verum* means true or genuine.

It is also known as *badian*, via the French *badiane*, which comes from the Chinese *bājiǎo*, literally eight horns, a description of its fruit as shown at the bottom of the image above.

Until 2012, Roche Pharmaceuticals used up to 90% of the world's annual star anise crop to produce *shikimic acid*, a chemical intermediate used in the synthesis of *oseltamivir*, sold under the brand name Tamiflu, an antiviral medication used to treat and prevent influenza A and influenza B, viruses that cause the flu.

Angelica (*Angelica officinalis*)

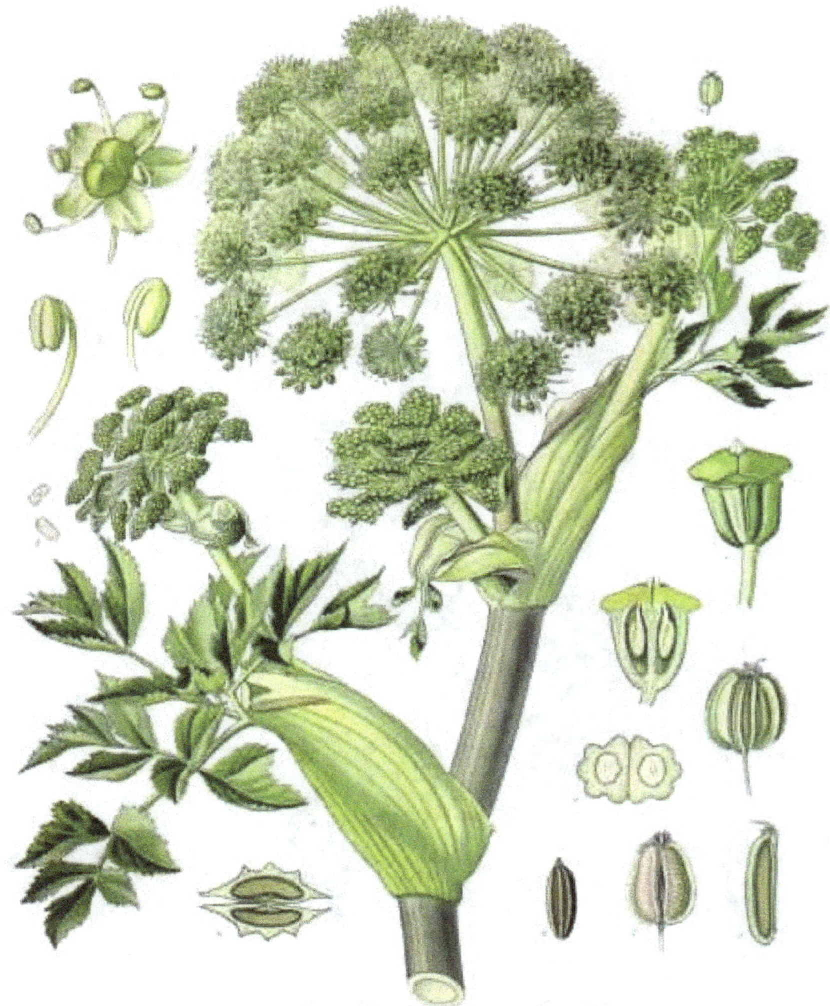

Angelica officinalis in Franz Eugen Köhler's *Medizinal-Pflanzen*, 1897

There are around 90 species of Angelica, and they are native to temperate and subarctic regions of the Northern Hemisphere as far north as Iceland, Lapland, and Greenland.

It is known for its sweetly scented edible stems and roots and is also called *Angelica archangelica*, *garden angelica*, *wild celery*, and *Norwegian angelica*. From the 10th century on, angelica was cultivated as a vegetable and medicinal plant, and achieved popularity in Scandinavia in the 12th century and is used especially in Sámi culture. It was once used as an herb in Sámi cooking, and known as *kvanne*.

Mainly found in China, it is grown traditionally for its medicinal properties and as a flavouring agent. Roots and seeds are commonly used to flavour gin and Chartreuse, Bénédictine, Vermouth, and Dubonnet.

Peppermint (*Mentha x piperita*)

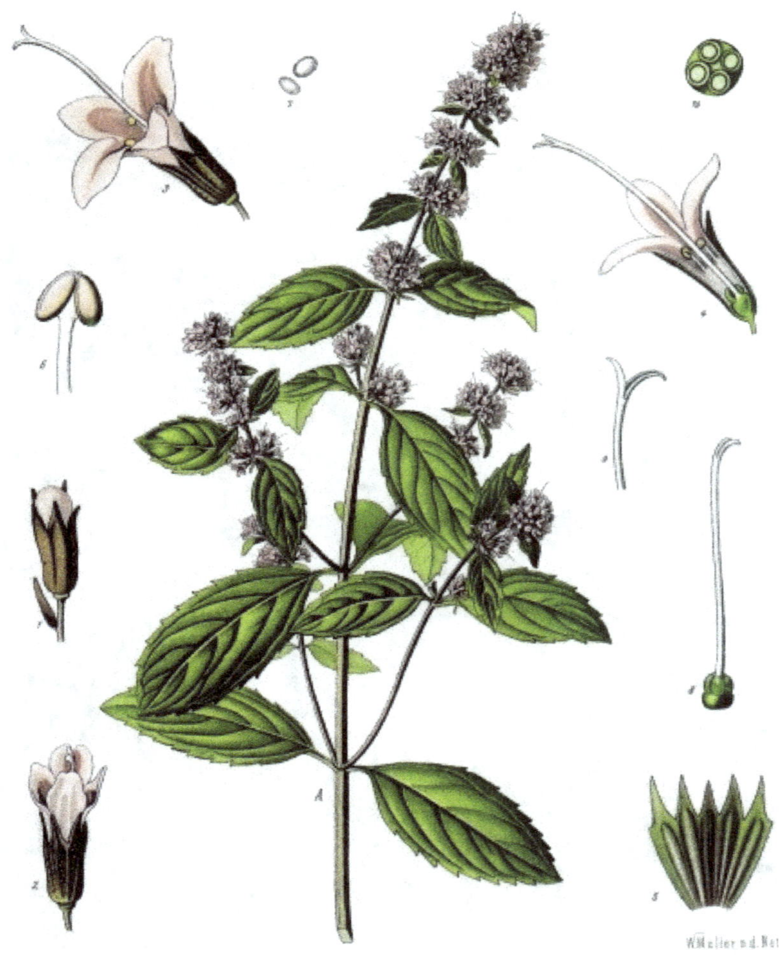

Mentha x piperita in Franz Eugen Köhler's *Medizinal-Pflanzen*, 1897

Peppermint is recognised as plant source of *menthol* and *menthone* and is among the oldest herbs used for food and medicine. Menthol activates cold-sensitive receptors in the skin and mucosal tissues, and is the primary source of the cooling sensation from the application of peppermint oil.

Peppermint oil has a high concentration of natural pesticides and is known to repel some pest insects such as mosquitoes and rodents. It has been used to relieve indigestion, improve brain function, decrease breastfeeding pain, improve cold symptoms, and kill bacteria which could result in bad breath.

Coriander (*Coriandrum sativum*)

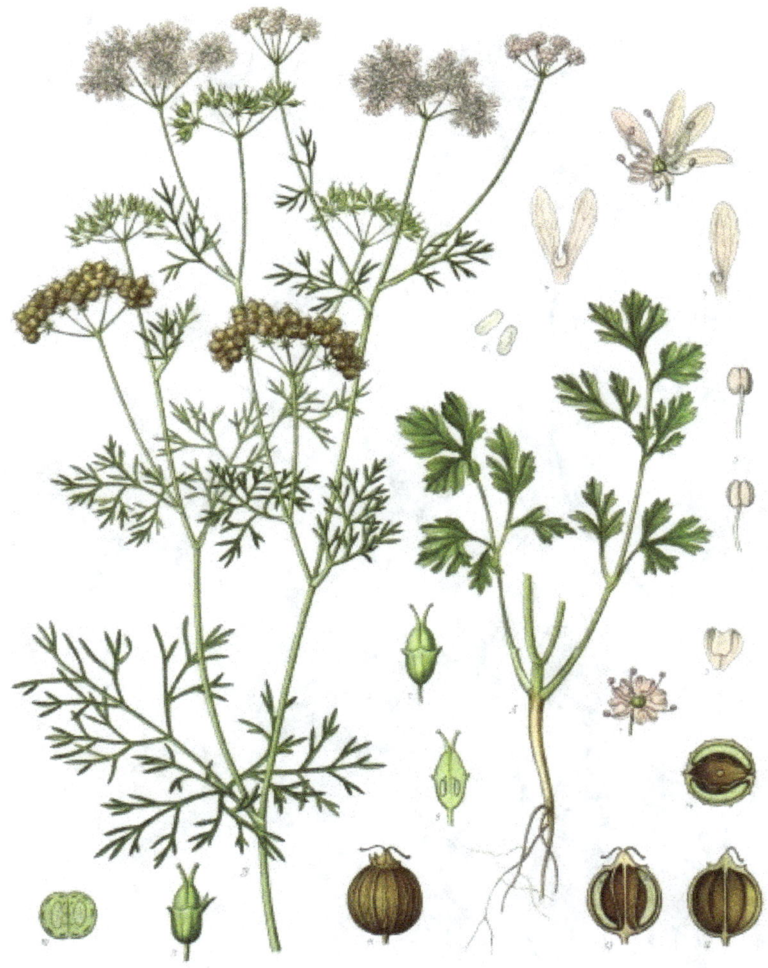

Coriandrum sativum in Franz Eugen Köhler's *Medizinal-Pflanzen*, 1897

Coriander entered English via the French *coriandre*, which comes from the Latin *coriandrum*, the Ancient Greek *κορίαννον koríannon* (or *κορίανδρον koríandron*). *Cilantro* is the Spanish word for coriander which also comes from the Latin *coriandrum*, and is a common term in American English due to their use in Mexican cuisine, where the seeds are still referred to as coriander.

The leaves and seeds of coriander have a distinctive citrus overtone. Fresh leaves and dried seeds are most commonly used in cooking, but all parts of the plant are edible. The roots are an important part of Thai cooking. Coriander is used in cuisines throughout the world. As heat diminishes their flavour, coriander leaves are often used raw or added to the dish immediately before serving. In Indian and Central Asian recipes, coriander leaves are used in large amounts and cooked until the flavour diminishes. The leaves spoil quickly when removed from the plant and lose their aroma when dried or frozen.

Veronica (*Veronica officinalis*)

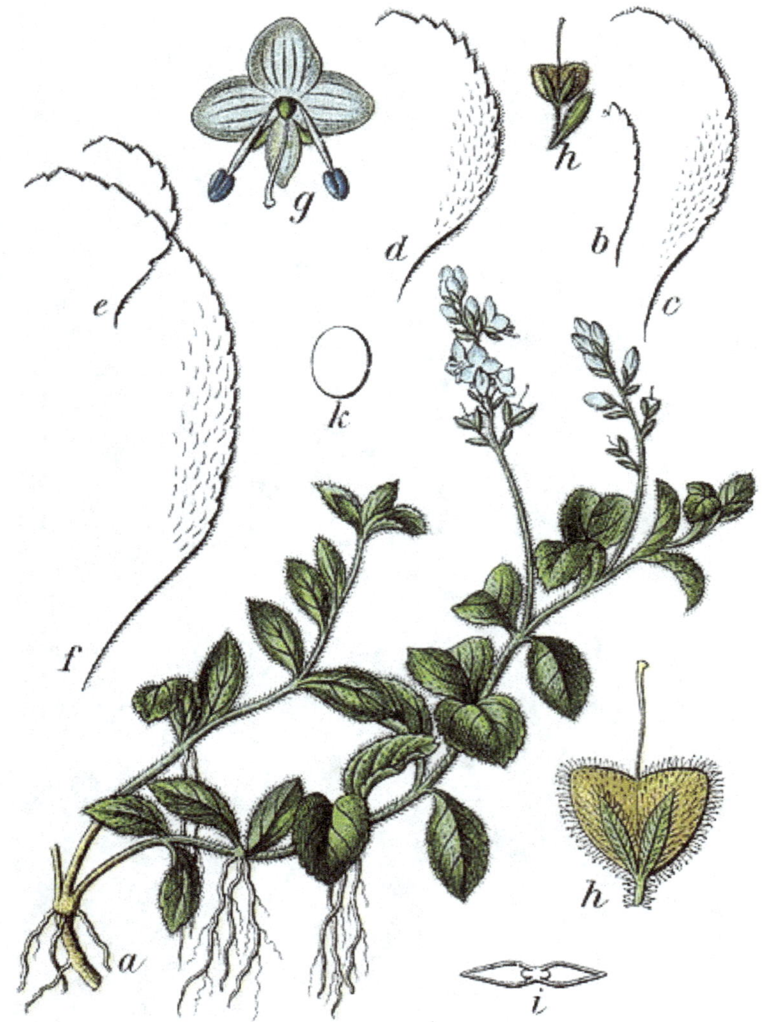

Veronica officinalis in Johann Georg Sturm's *Deutschlands Flora in Abbildungen*, 1796

Veronica has over four hundred species and hybrids, also known as *speedwell*, *bird's eye*, and *gypsyweed*. It has been used medicinally as an expectorant, served in tea to alleviate bronchial congestion associated with asthma and allergies.

It is also used as a tea in traditional Austrian medicine as a treatment for disorders of the nervous system, respiratory tract, cardiovascular system, and metabolism.

It is reported to have a flavour similar to watercress, slightly acidic or bitter, which contributes to the overall bitterness in the complex herbal profile of absinthe.

3.   Absinthium: The Ancient Green Wonder

Humans have been using plants for medicinal purposes as far back as Palaeolithic times, approximately 60,000 years ago. Plant samples from prehistoric burial sites have supported the idea that Palaeolithic people had knowledge of herbal medicine. For example, large amounts of pollen from 8 plant species have been found at a 60,000 year old Neanderthal burial site in northern Iraq, and 7 of these plant species are now used as herbal remedies. In one of the cradles of civilisation, the Fertile Crescent of Mesopotamia (5500 to 1800 BCE), the Sumerians created clay tablets with lists of plants and their medicinal uses.

Medicinal herbs were found in the personal effects of *Ötzi the Iceman*, whose body was frozen in the Ötztal Alps for more than 5,000 years until his discovery in 1991. These herbs appear to have been used to treat the parasites found in his intestines. *Artemisia absinthium* is one of the many plants historically used as a medicine against parasitic worms, gnats, fleas, moths, pains, and fevers.

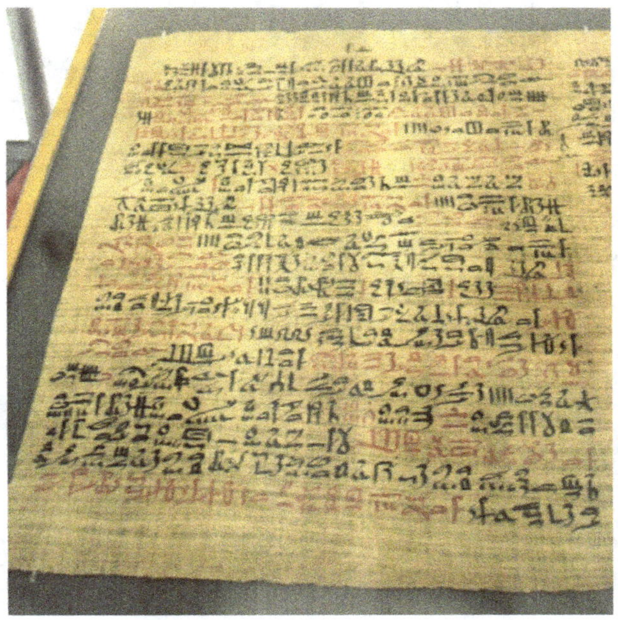

The **Ebers Papyrus**[1] (left) is an Ancient Egyptian medical document containing knowledge of herbs, plants, and their medicinal uses, dating to around 1550 BCE.

If the translation for wormwood is correct, it contains 15 herbal remedies that use wormwood, taken internally as a food, a drink (sometimes combined with beer), or suppository for abdominal complaints, constipation, coughing, digestive tract complaints, parasitic worms, general protection, and vomiting, and taken externally as an ointment for skin disease, and for diseases of the mouth by something called the *sechep method*.

Other than papyri, evidence of herbal medicine has also been found in tomb illustrations or jars containing traces of herbs.

The Ebers Papyrus remedy no. Eb 100 (24, 18- 24, 20) reads:

> "Another (remedy) ⟨for⟩ killing agents of disease in the abdomen: Course ground sut emmer: 300 cm³, course ground barley: 300 cm³, crushed dates: 75 cm³, shenfet fruit: 37.5 cm³, shredded dates: 75 cm³, two halves of a pesedj pod: 75 cm³, wormwood: 37.5 cm³. To be cooked; (and) left overnight for condensation to form. To be drunk over 4 days."

Wormwood extracts and wine-soaked wormwood leaves were used as remedies by the ancient Greeks, and some evidence exists of a wormwood-flavoured wine in ancient Greece called *absinthites oinos*. The Greek physician **Hippocrates** (c460-370 BCE), often referred to as the father of medicine, recommended wormwood for jaundice, tetanus, and stimulating menstruation in the form of a bitter tea. It was also used as a cure for indigestion, gastritis, and other peptic ailments.

---

[1] (n.d.). *The Ebers Papyrus. The Ebers Papyrus*. Retrieved January 23, 2024, from https://papyrusebers.de/

Theophrastus (371-287 BCE) was a Greek philosopher who in his botanical work *Historia Plantarum* associated wormwood with the Greek words *ápsinthos* = unpleasant, disagreeable, or *ápinthos* = unfit for drinking.

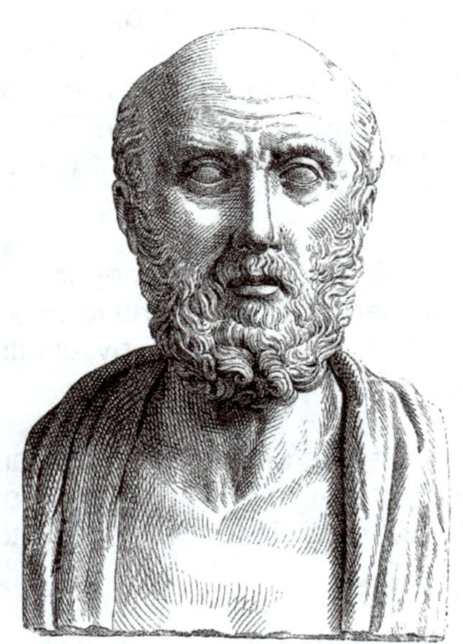

Hippocrates
19th century engraving of a
Roman bust

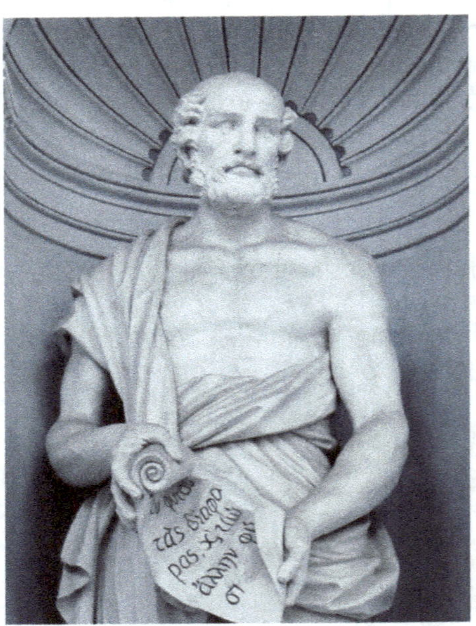

Theophrastus
Statue, Palermo Botanical
Garden

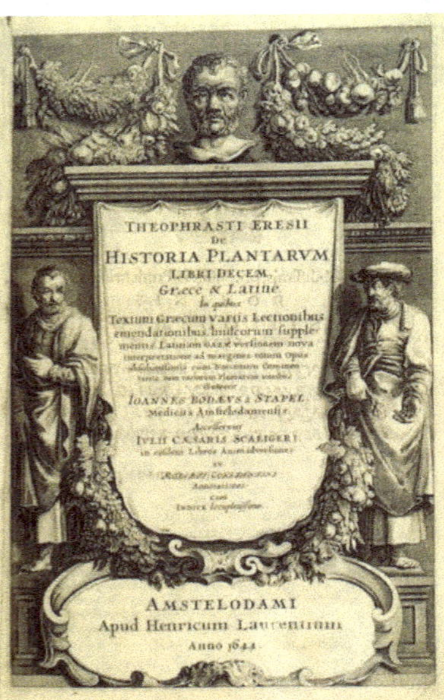

Historia Plantarum, 1644

In the Germanic literature on herbal medicine, the name *wermut* appears, indicating the antiparasitic effect of this herb attributed to its bitter taste (*werm* in Old German means worm).

Lucretius (99-55 BCE) was a Roman poet and a philosopher. He wrote the philosophical poem *De Rerum Natura* (The Nature of Things) which was designed to introduce Roman readers to Epicurean philosophy and physics through the medium of richly poetic language and metaphors. In this work he mentions the practice of lining the rim of a cup with honey to take away the bitter taste of absinthia for children:

"nam vel uti pueris absinthia taetra medentes cum dare conantur, prius oras pocula circum contingunt mellis dulci flavoque liquore, ut puerorum aetas inprovida ludificetur labrorum tenus, interea perpotet amarum absinthi laticem deceptaque non capiatur, sed potius tali facto recreata valescat"

"for even when they are trying to give the children the offensive absinthe, they first touch the rims of the cups with honey, a sweet yellow liquid, so that the unprepared age of the children may play with the tight lips, while in the meantime the bitter absinthe may pass through the latex and not be deceived, but rather be refreshed by such a deed"

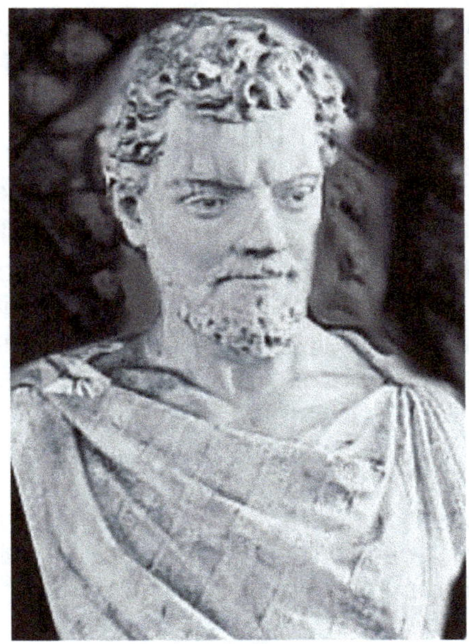

Lucretius
by Parco del Pincio, c1859-1861

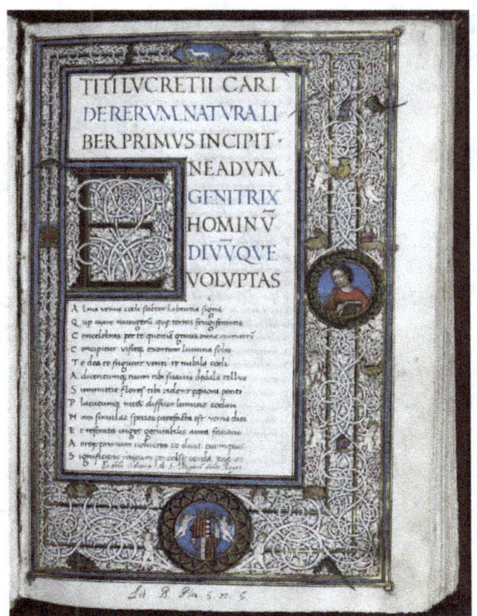

De Rerum Natura
c1475-1494

The Roman encyclopaedist **Celsus** (25 BCE-50 CE) in his *De Medicina* suggests absinth with honey as part of a cure for urinary tract infections:

"Adversus urinae difficultatem piperis longi, castorei, murrae, galbani, papaveris lacrimae, croci, costi uncia singulae; styracis, resinae terebenthinae pondo sextantes, melabsinthi cyathus. Ex quibus ad magnitudinem fabae Aegyptiae et mane et cenato dari debet"

"For difficult micturition long pepper, castory, myrrh, galbanum, poppy-tears, saffron, costmary, 28 grams each; storax and turpentine-resin, 56 grams each, honey with absinth 42 cc. Of this an amount the size of an Egyptian bean should be taken in the morning and after dinner"

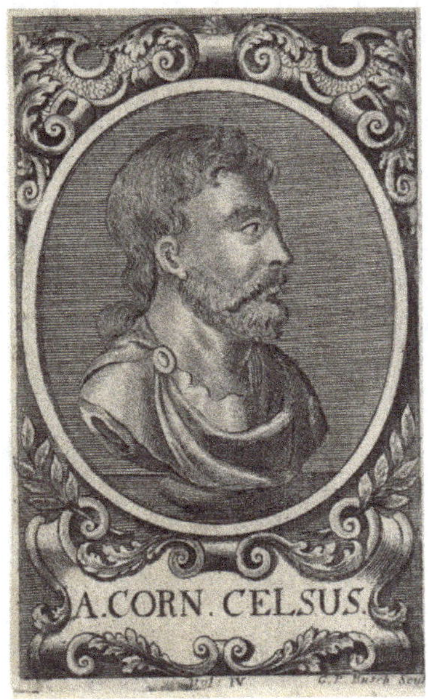

Celsus
Georg P Busch, 1719

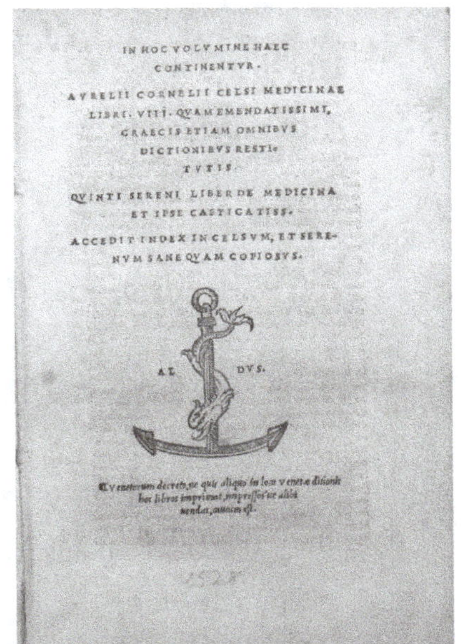

De Medicina, 1528

Pliny the Elder (c23-79 CE) was a Roman author, naturalist, natural philosopher, and a naval and army commander in the early Roman Empire. In around 77-79 CE, he wrote the encyclopaedic *Naturalis Historiae*:

"Absinthii genera plura sunt: Santonicum appellatur e Galliae civitate, Ponticum e Ponto, ubi pecora pinguescunt illo et ob id sine felle reperiuntur, neque aliud praestantius, multoque Italicum amarius, sed medulla Pontici dulcis. de usu eius convenit, herbae facillimae atque inter paucas utilissimae, praeterea sacris populi Romani celebratae peculiariter, siquidem Latinarum feriis quadrigae certant in Capitolio victorque absinthium bibit, credo, sanitatem praemio dari honorifice arbitratis maioribus

"There are several kinds of absinthe: it is called Santonicum from the city of Gaul, Ponticum from Pontus, where the cattle are fattened by it and for that reason they are found without hides, and nothing else is more excellent, and much more bitter than the Italian, but the sweet marrow of Ponticus. it is agreed upon its use, the easiest and among the few most useful herbs, moreover, especially celebrated as sacred by the Roman people, for on the Latin holidays the teams compete in the Capitol, and the victor drinks absinthe, I believe, and health is awarded as a prize to honourable judges of the elders

stomachum corroborat, et ob hoc sapor eius in vina transfertur, ut diximus. bibitur et decoctum aqua ac postea nocte et die refrigeratum sub diu; decoci VI drachmis foliorum cum ramis suis in caelestis aquae sextariis III oportet, nec non salem addi vetustissimi usus est. bibitur et madefacti dilutum; ita enim appelletur hoc genus. diluti ratio ut, quisquis fuerit modus aquae, tegatur per triduum"

it strengthens the stomach, and for this reason its flavour is transferred to the wines, as we have said. it is drunk and boiled with water, and then cooled at night and day under a long time; It is necessary to decoction 6 drachms of the leaves with their branches in 3 sextars of celestial water, and also to add salt. it is drunk and diluted; for this kind is so called. the method of diluting, so that, whatever the mode of the water, it is covered for three days"

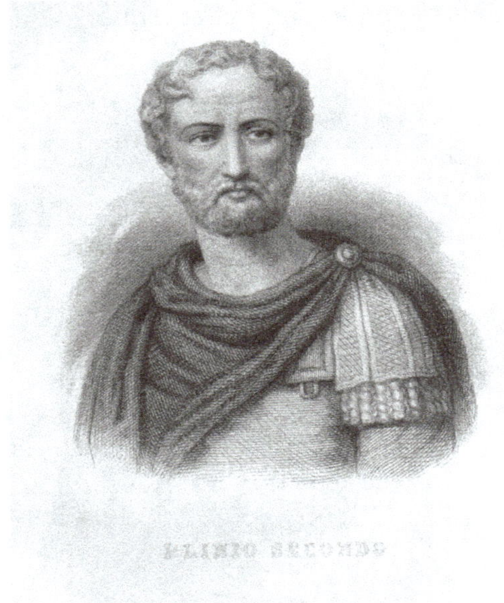

Pliny the Elder
Illustration, 1859

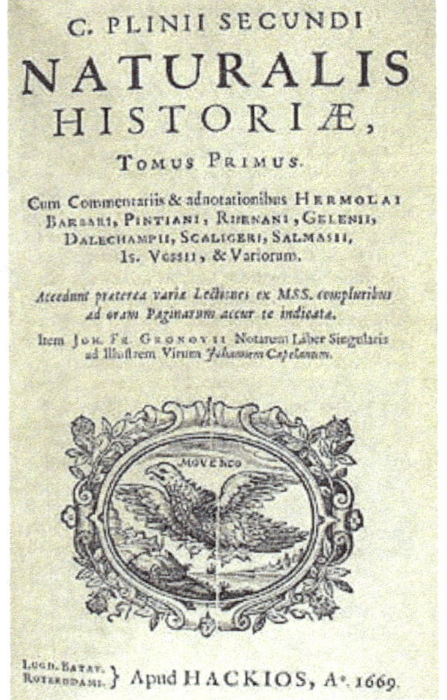

Naturalis Historiae, 1669

Greek physician, pharmacologist, and botanist **Dioscorides** (40-90 CE), suggests in his *De Materia Medica* that absinthium is helpful in treating complaints affecting the digestive tract:

"Absinthium amarissimum [quod Aegyptii somi, rusticum absinthium Romani vocant] herba est vulgo cognita. … Vim habet calefacientem, astingentem, concoctioni faventem biliosaque detrahentem, quae stomacho alvoque inhaerescunt"

"Absinthium, the very bitter one [the Egyptians call it Somi, the Romans Rusticum Absinthium], is a commonly-known herb. … It has the power to warm, astringent, promote digestion, and cleanse the stomach and abdomen of bilious substances that have penetrated into it"

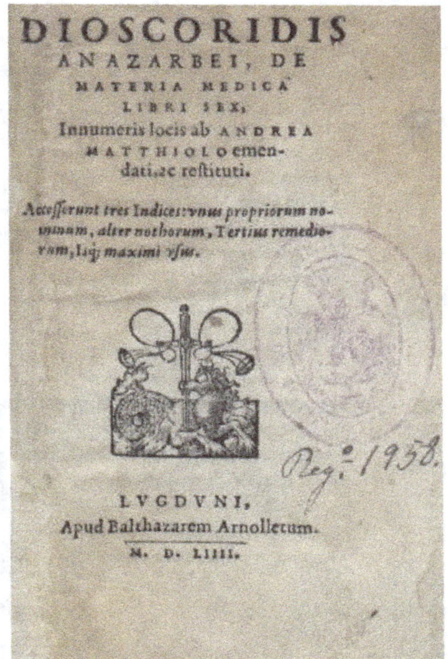

Dioscorides
Juliana Anicia Codex, c512

De Materia Medica, 1553

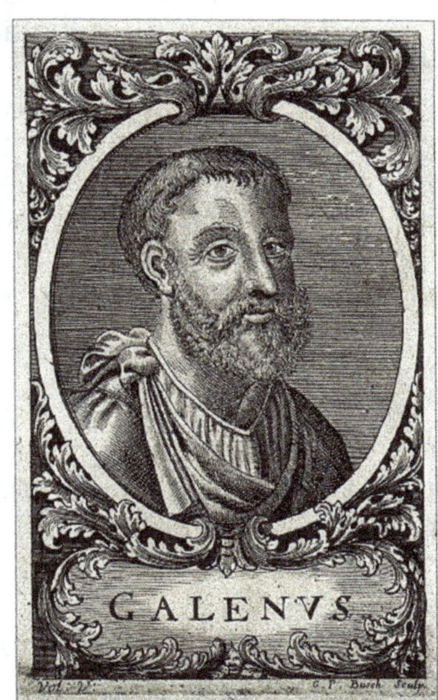

Galen (129-216 CE) was a Roman-Greek physician, surgeon, and philosopher. He is widely considered to be one of the most accomplished of all medical researchers of antiquity.

He influenced the development of several fields of science, anatomy, physiology, pathology, pharmacology, and neurology.

In his *De Simplicibus Medicaminibus* (6.1.75), describes wormwood as astringent, bitter and pungent. Therefore, it has a warming, cleaning, tonic, and dehydrating action. It is warming at the 1st degree and dehydrating at the 3rd. Thanks to this, it eliminates the excess of bile in the digestive and circulatory systems.

Left: Galen, by Georg P Busch, 18th century

Zhang Zhongjing (150-219) was a Chinese pharmacologist, physician, inventor, and writer during the Eastern Han dynasty. In his *Shanghan lun* (Treatise on Febrile Diseases) he describes a medicinal soup containing wormwood.

茵陳蒿湯方

茵陳蒿六兩　梔子十四枚（擘）　大黃二兩（去皮）

上三味，以水一斗二升，先煮茵陳減六升

內二味，煮取三升，去滓，分三服。

Yinchen Artemesia Soup Recipe

6 taels of Artemisia wormwood, 14 pieces of gardenia (broken), 2 taels of rhubarb (peeled)

For the three flavours, use one bucket and two litres of water, boil the wormwood first and reduce it by six litres.

For the second flavour, boil three litres, drain and divide into three servings.

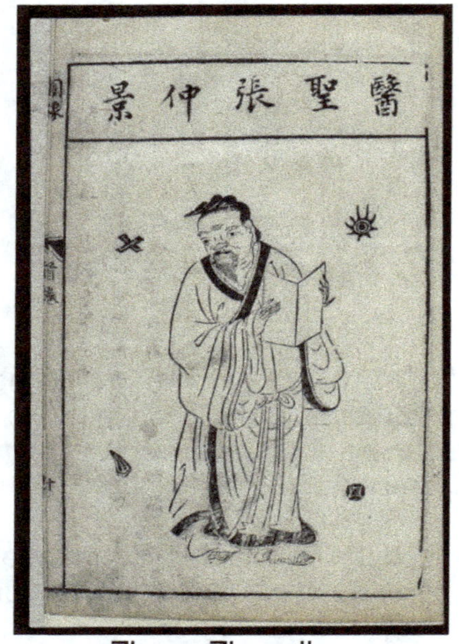

Zhang Zhongjing
by Gan Bozong, Ming Dynasty c1573-1620

The history of Ancient Chinese medicine begins with the mythological Yan (flame) Emperor Shennong or who lived around 2800 BCE. He has become a deity in Chinese folk religion as the Divine Farmer.

Legend says that he taught the Chinese people how to farm, and how to use plants for medicine. The *Shennong Bencaojing* is a collection of agricultural and medicinal knowledge attributed to this mythical Emperor.

He is credited with the discovery that sweet wormwood cures malaria. Researchers believe this text was collected from ancient oral tradition and finally written down during the Eastern Han Dynasty, sometime between 206 BCE and 220 CE.

Hunayn ibn Ishaq (808-873), also known as **Joannitius**, was an Arabic translator, scholar, physician, and scientist. He was active during the *Islamic Golden Age*, a period of economic and cultural flourishing that prioritised the collection of knowledge. He worked with a group of fellow scholars translating books of philosophy and classical Greek and Persian texts.

These texts were influential in the Islamic world, notably to the Persian philosopher and physician **Ibn Sina** (980-1037), also known in the West as **Avicenna**. In his work *Al-Qanun fi't-Tibb* (The Canon of Medicine) he mentions several species of wormwood growing eastwards up to Khorasan (present day Afghanistan, Turkmenistan, and Iran). He described it as similar to oregano, bitter, acrid, and astringent. He passes on the treatments suggested by Galen, but also adds it as a possible treatment of alopecia, dark circles under the eyes, and for giving a good colour to the skin.

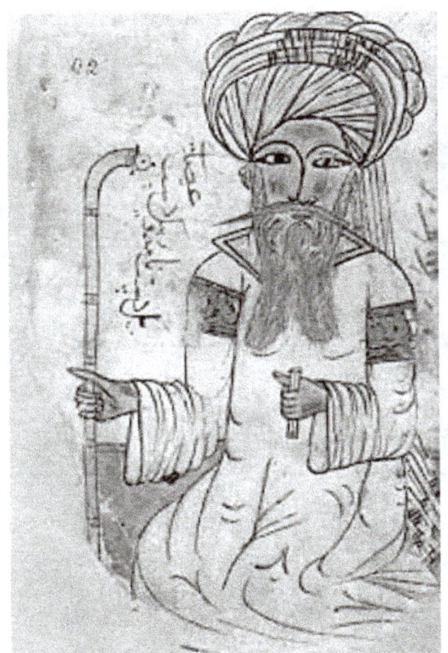

Avicenna, from the medieval manuscript
Subtleties of Truth, 1271

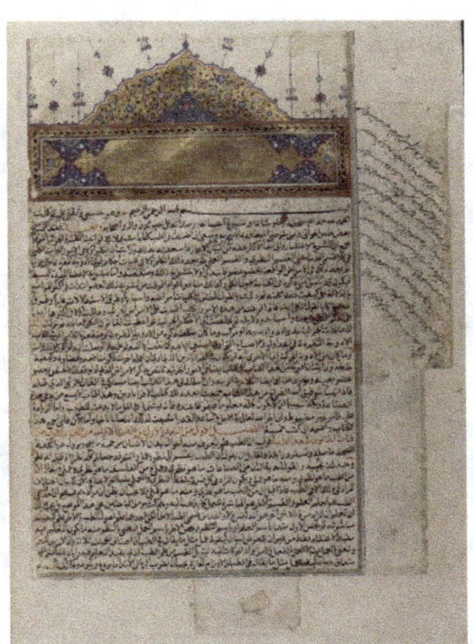

The Canon of Medicine, 16th century

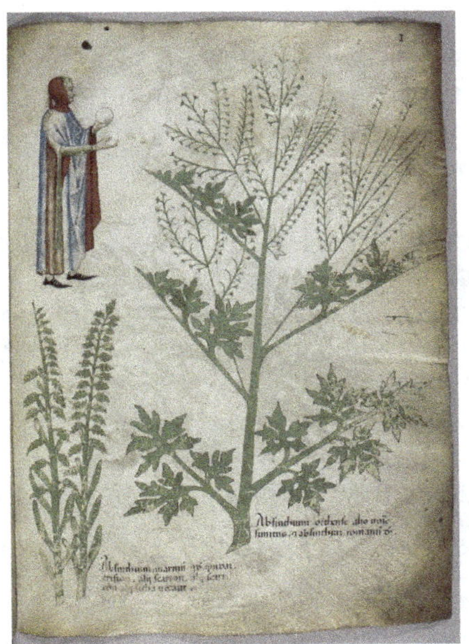

The translation of Greek and Latin texts into Arabic helped to preserve them and prevent their collected knowledge from being lost in the periods of upheaval and political changes in the Late Middle Ages.

Translations from Arabic into Latin arrived in Europe via Italy and were compiled into encyclopaedias and compendia.

One of these is the so-called **Tractatus de Herbis** (Treatise on Herbs), dating back to the 13th century, with images designed to avoid confusion in the identification of plants and to clear up any errors in translation.

Left: *Absinthium*, in *Tractatus de Herbis*, c1440, Sloane MS 4016, British Library, London

Paracelsus (1493-1541) (Theophrastus von Hohenheim) was a Swiss physician, alchemist, lay theologian, and philosopher of the German Renaissance. He was a pioneer of the so-called medical revolution of the Renaissance, combining observations with received wisdom. He is also called the father of toxicology.

He is credited with inventing or at least naming a kind of liniment, embrocation, or heat rub called Opodeldoc. It is a mixture of soap in alcohol, which then has camphor and herbal essences added, including wormwood. He mentions it in his work *Bertheonea Sive Chirurgia Minor* published after his death in 1603, but with some of the ingredients left uncertain.

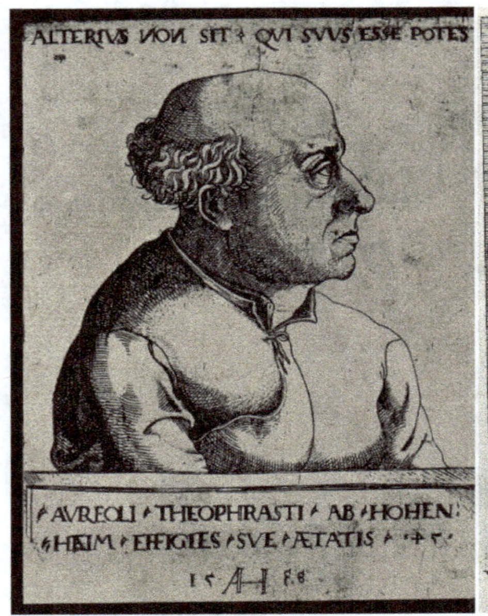
Paracelsus
by Augustin Hirschvogel, 1538

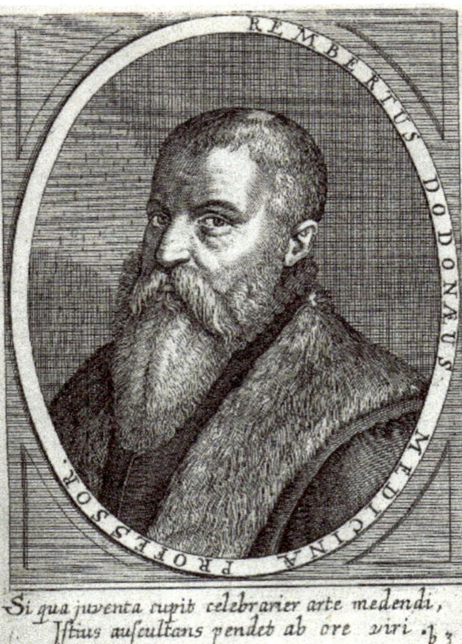
Dodoens
by Theodor de Bry, in
Bibliotheca chalcographica,1669

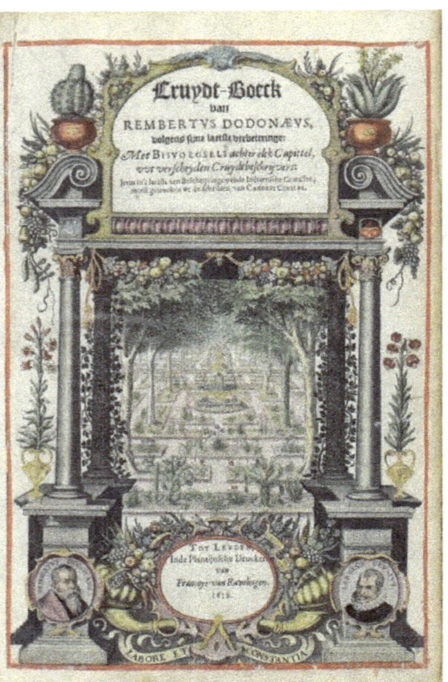
Cruydt-Boek, 1618

Rembert Dodoens (1517-1585) was a Flemish physician. His *Cruydt-Boek* (Herb-Book) of 1554 built on the work of Dioscorides and Galen, including around 515 illustrations from the 1543 work *New-Kreuterbüchlein* (New Herb Book) of **Leonhart Fuchs** (1501-1566). Dodoens distinguished five different species of wormwood:

- One, with large leaves (*latifolium*), which corresponded to the Pontic species of Dioscorides, and was found in some cold mountains of Switzerland
- Two, the marine species, with narrow leaves called *Seriphon*, the second species of Dioscorides, growing on the shores of Holland, Zeeland, and Flanders, and in France and Italy
- Three, the Egyptian species
- Four, the narrow-leaf species, which grew in Mysia (Asia Minor), Thracia (north-east Greece), and Pannonia (north-eastern Greece and Bulgaria), and also in Bohemia, Germany, Belgium, and England, commonly designated as the Roman Absinth. (the same species as the Pontic described by Galen)
- Five, a scented and tasteless species

John Gerard (ca 1545-1612) was an English herbalist. In his *Generall Historie of Plantes* published in 1597 he disagrees with one of Galen's claims of absinthium, stating:

> *"It is very profitable to a weak stomach that is troubled with choler, for it cleanseth it through his bitterness, purgeth by siege and urine: by reason of the binding quality, it strengtheneth and comorteth the stomach, but helpeth nothing at all to remove phlegm contained in the stomach, as Galen addeth"*

He also recommends its use as moth repellent for clothing and an ointment for repelling gnats:

> *"it keepeth garments also from the moths, it driveth away gnats, the body being anointed with the oil thereof".*

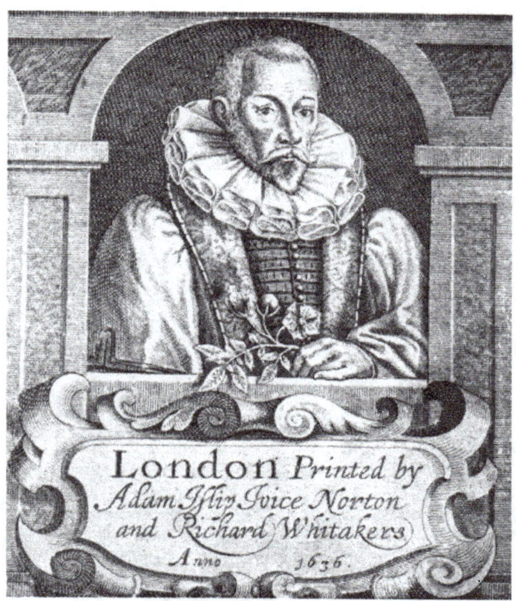

John Gerard
Generall Historie of Plantes, 1636

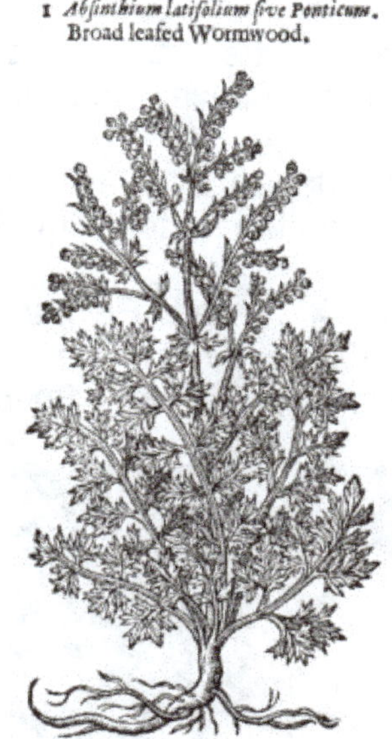

Broad-Leaved Wormwood
Absinthium Latifolium

In 1633 **Thomas Johnson** (c1595-1644) published a version of John Gerard's work with a large number of amendments and additional species and images, reflecting the great progress that had been made in the field of botany in the 36 years since its first publication.

Nicholas Culpeper (1616-1654) was an English botanist, herbalist, physician and astrologer who assigned astrological figures to herbs as part of his philosophy. In his book *The English Physitian* of 1652 he describes Wormwood as a herb of Mars. He philosophises that different varieties of wormwood should be used depending on their strength, for example Seriphian wormwood is weaker and therefore better suited to children and those of a ripe age, and common wormwood which is stronger should be used for others. He goes on to suggest that for those that live near the sea, Seriphian wormwood is better suited to them because it is nourished by the same air.

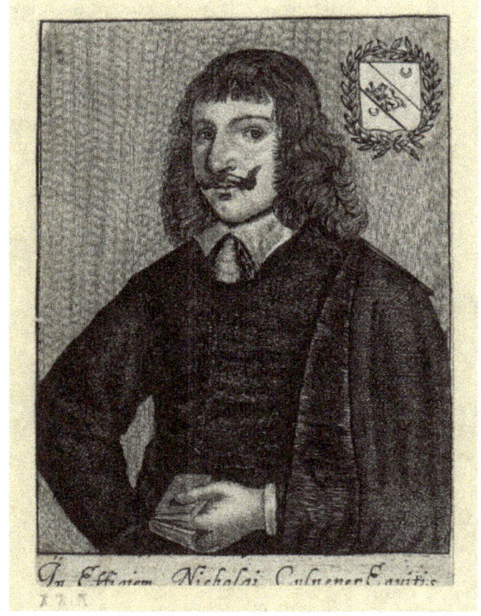

Nicholas Culpeper
by Richard Gaywood, c1664-1662

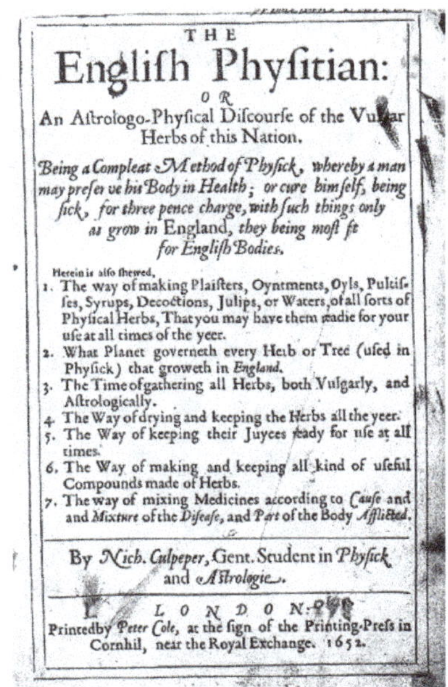

The English Physitian, 1652

By the 18th century the amount of collected knowledge on plants and medicine became so great that it needed to be systematically classified and catalogued.

This was undertaken by **Carl Linnaeus** (1707-1778), a Swedish biologist and a physician who became known as the father of modern botany.

In his 1742 work *Genera Plantarum* (Types of Plants) placed Artemisia Absinthium into *Class XIX Syngenesia*, Order *Polygamia Superflua*. By its fifth edition *Genera Plantarum* served as a compendium to his 1753 work *Species Plantarum* (Species of Plants).

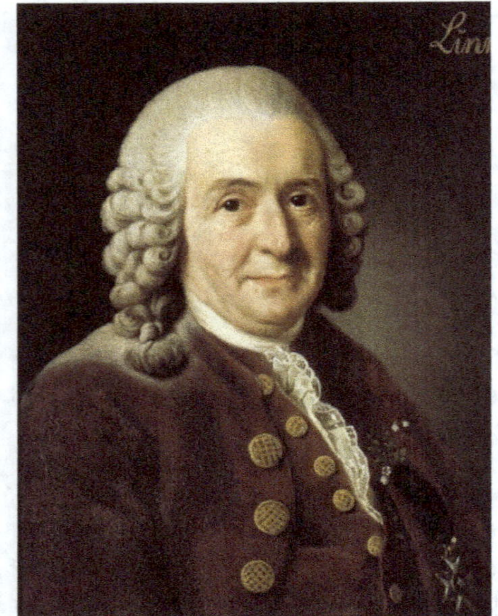

Carl Linnaeus
by Alexander Roslin, 1775

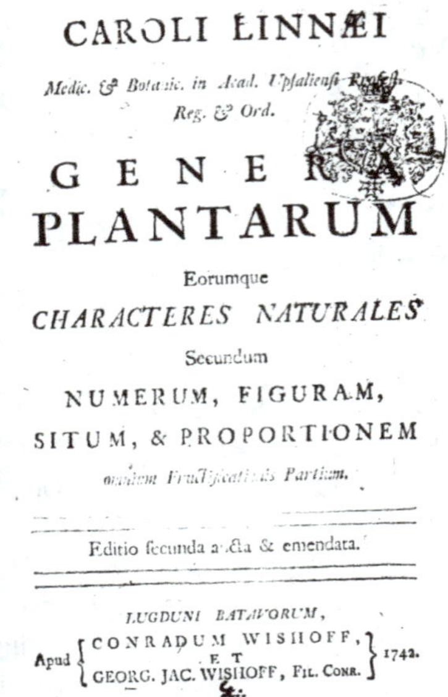

Genera Plantarum, 1742

398 SYNGENESIA POLYGAMIA SUPERFLUA.

779. ARTEMISIA*. *Tournef.* 260. *Vaill.* A. G. 1719. f. 23. 31. 36. 45. Abrotanum *Tournef.* Abfinthium *Tournef.* 260. *Vaill.* A. G. 1719. f. 32.

CAL. *Communis* fubrotundus, imbricatus: *fquamis* rotundatis, conniventibus.
COR. compofita: *corollulæ bermapbroditæ* tubulofæ, plures, in difco. *Femininæ* petalis ferme nudæ, in ambitu. *Propria Hermapbroditi* infundibuliformis: *limbo* quinquefido.
STAM. Hermaphroditis *Filamenta* quinque, capillaria, breviffima. *Antbera* cylindracea, tubulofa, quinquedentata.
PIST. Hermaphroditis *Germen* parvum. *Stylus* filiformis, longitudine ftaminum. *Stigma* bifidum, revolutum. Feminis *Germen* minimum. *Stylus* filiformis, hermaphroditis longior. *Stigma* hermaphroditis fimile.
PER. nullum. *Calyx* vix mutatus.
SEM. *Hermapbroditis* folitaria, nuda. *Feminis* folitaria, nuda.
REC. planum, nudum, aut villofum.
OBS. Abfinthium T. *Receptaculo villofo gaudet, & calyce magis globofo.* Abrotonum T. *Receptaculo eft nudo.* Artemifia T. *Receptaculo etiam eft nudo.* Seriphium Pn. *Receptaculo nudo; feminulis nullis.* Breyniana Pt. *Calyce uniflora.*

Artemisia Absinthium
Genera Plantarum, 2nd edition,
1742, p398

By the end of the 18th century absinthium had become a well-used allegory for bitterness, hence the phrase 'bitter as wormwood'.

4.   Absinthe: Elixir, Aperitif, Art and Poetry

Absinthium has an incredibly long history with wide range of medicinal uses, and herbal remedies have been prepared and served through the ages by healers, monks, and physicians alike.

The evolutionary path of absinthe is similar to that of tea and coffee. First a medicine, then a luxury product with health benefits, enjoyed by the wealthy, then enjoyed by the middle classes, then enjoyed by everyone as an affordable leisure item, and finally part of a national cultural identity.

At around 1792 in Couvet, Switzerland, French doctor Pierre Ordinaire[23] is credited with having created an all-purpose patent remedy for the treatment of epilepsy, gout, kidney stones, colic, headaches, and worms etc., known as *Extrait d'Absinthe* (Extract of Absinthe) nicknamed *La Fée Verte* (The Green Fairy).

It is also possible that this version of events has been somewhat embellished over time, and that he did not necessarily create it but was well known in the region as a doctor who did much to promote it.

This recipe was passed from Dr Ordinaire's governess to the Henriod sisters of Couvet, who along with others had long been making medicinal tinctures as far back at least as the 1750s, where it was sold as a medicinal elixir.

In 1797 the Swiss businessman Daniel-Henri Dubied became interested in this elixir, seeing its potential not just as a patent medicine, but as an aperitif. He then purchased the formula from the Henriod sisters and opened the first absinthe distillery named *Dubied Père et Fils* in Couvet with his son Marcellin and son-in-law Henry-Louis Pernod.

In 1805 they had a second larger distillery built in Pontarlier, France under the name Maison Pernod Fils run by Henri-Louis Pernod.

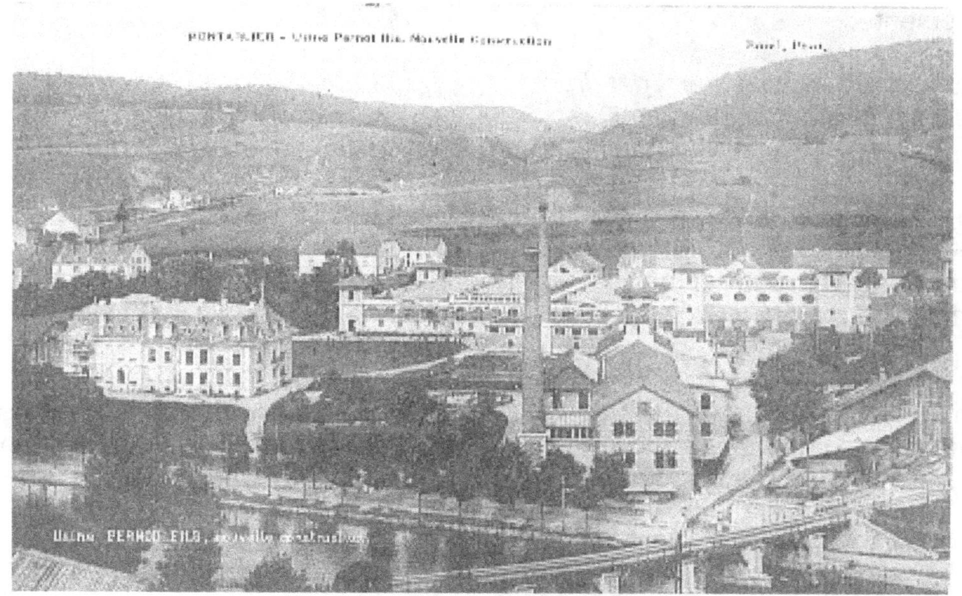

The Pernod Fils factory, 1905

[2] Wittels, Betina J.; Hermesch, Robert (2003). *Absinthe: Sip of Seduction. Speck Press. ISBN 978-0-9725776-1-8.*
[3] Wittels, Betina; Breaux, T. A. (2017-06-06). *Absinthe: The Exquisite Elixir. Fulcrum Publishing. ISBN 978-1-68275-156-5.*

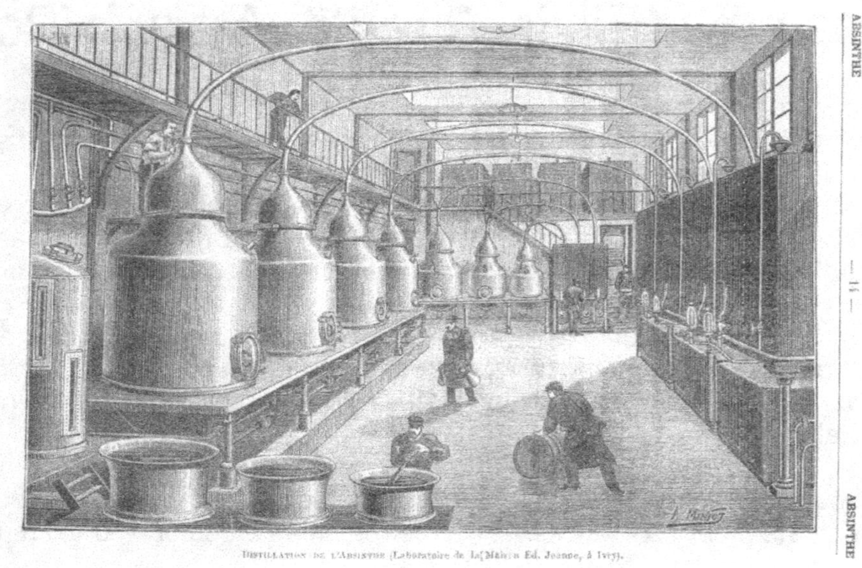

Distillation De l'Absinthe (Laboratorie de la Maison Ed. Joanne, a Ivry), 1904

The popularity of the Pernod Fils brand grew steadily in the following decades, and the formerly sleepy community of Pontarlier would eventually become home to 28 commercial absinthe distilleries, making it the world's centre of absinthe production, thought of by many as the spiritual home of absinthe producing as much as 30,000 litres a day.

The English poet **Lord Byron** (1788-1824) is often mentioned in lists of 'famous absinthe drinkers'. In 1816 he left England and journeyed through Belgium, settling in Villa Diodati by Lake Geneva, Switzerland. It is here that Byron would certainly have become accustomed to absinthe and its traditions, particularly in the company of Madame de Staël, a prominent woman of letters and a political theorist well known in the intellectual circles of Paris and Geneva, and a champion of the Romantic movement.

> *"Man, being reasonable, must get drunk;*
> *The best of life is but intoxication"*
>
> *Lord Byron, Don Juan (1819-24) canto 2, st. 179*

Another name that appears frequently on 'famous absinthe drinkers' lists is **Edgar Allen Poe** (1809-1849), an American writer, poet, author, editor, and literary critic. He is well known for his tales of mystery and the macabre and for being a central figure of the Romantic movement and of Gothic fiction in American literature.

By association with Romanticism, Gothic fiction, and the macabre, the general feeling that Poe *must* have been a heavy absinthe drinker has been enough to convince public consciousness that he was. There is no evidence to support this idea, nothing is mentioned in any of his books or correspondence, there are no contemporary reports, and absinthe only became widely available in the United States after his death.

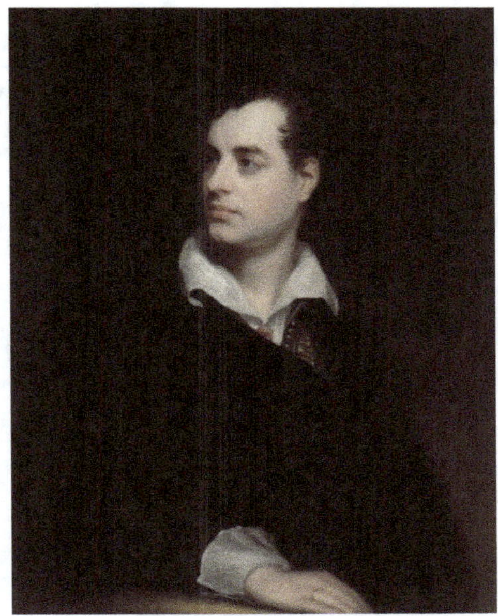

Lord Byron
by Thomas Phillips, 1813

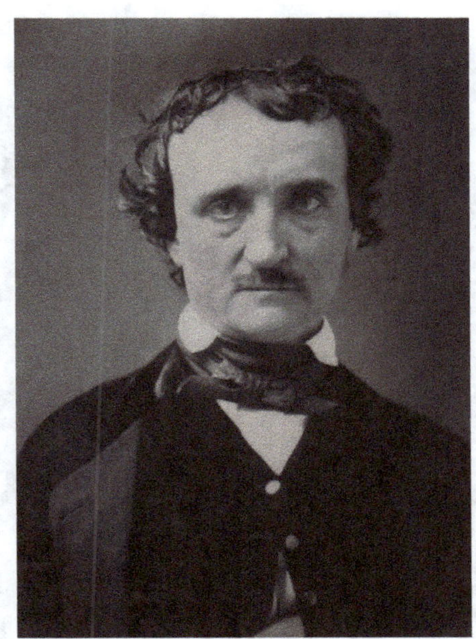

Edgar Allen Poe
unknown photographer, c1849

In the 1840s, absinthe was given to French troops fighting in Algeria to prevent malaria and fevers, kill germs, and fend off dysentery. It was mixed with water or wine and colloquially referred to as absinthe soup. When the troops of the *Bataillon d'Afrique* returned to France, they brought their taste for absinthe back with them, requesting it in bars, bistros, and cafés, all over France.

The tradition of beginning a meal with an *aperitif* (opener) to sharpen the appetite became well established by this time. There were hundreds of different liqueurs and spirits available with similar local and regional herbs and ingredients, and absinthe enjoyed an ever increasing share of the aperitifs that were drunk.

With the increase in popularity of absinthe came an increase in production, which made it more affordable until it was enjoyed by more and more people across all walks of society. Relaxed licensing laws in the 1860s resulted in more drinking establishments opening, and by 1869 more than 30,000 existed in Paris alone, particularly in the district of Montmartre. In almost all of them, 5pm became known as *l'heure verte* (the green hour[4]).

The rise in café culture provided people with a space to socialise, and an escape the harsh realities of everyday life. Many of Paris' citizens were living in cramped apartments, often in squalor and poverty.

Charles Baudelaire (1821-1867) commented on the social change and rapid industrialisation of cities like Paris in his 1857 work *Les Fleurs du Mal* (The Flowers of Evil). He explored themes of decadence, suffering, immorality, and the excesses of absinthe among other substances, as a temporary escape from harsh realities and self-loathing. In the poem *Le Poison* he mused:

"Tout cela ne vaut pas le poison qui découle
De tes yeux, de tes yeux verts,
Lacs où mon âme tremble et se voit à l'envers...

Mes songes viennent en foule
Pour se désaltérer à ces gouffres amers"

"All that is not equal to the poison which flows
From your eyes, from your green eyes,
Lakes where my soul trembles and sees its evil side...
My dreams come in multitude
To slake their thirst in those bitter gulfs"

---

[4] St. Clair, Kassia (2016). *The Secret Lives of Colour.* London: John Murray. p. 217. ISBN 978-1473630819. OCLC 936144129.

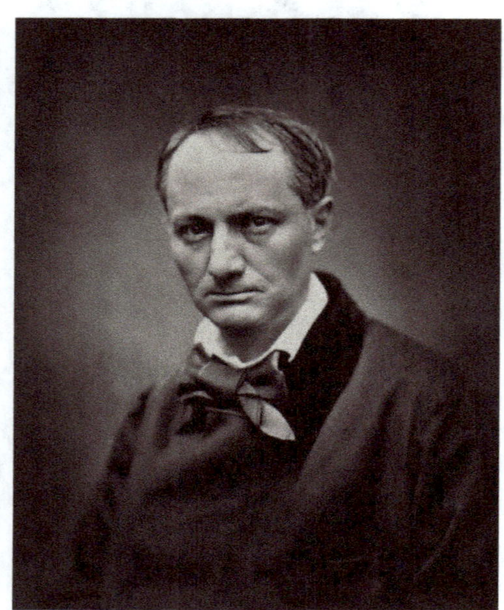
Charles Baudelaire
by Étienne Carjat, 1862

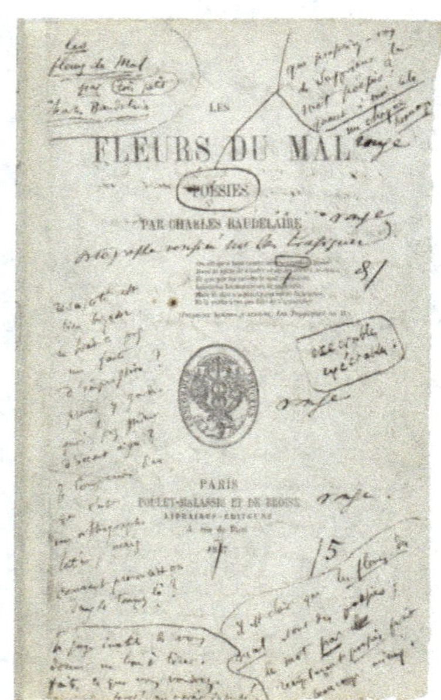
Les Fleurs du Mal
First edition with author's notes

By this time, the phenomenon of the salon as a social and cultural event was already well established in France. The Salon de Paris was the official art exhibition of the *Académie des Beaux-Arts* (Academy of Fine Arts) which dominated French art.

It showcased the selected works of painters, sculptors, architects, engravers, musicians and composers. Those that were judged to be acceptable within the conservative values of the academy won prizes, earned commissions, and enhanced their prestige. The so called Salon music of Frédéric Chopin, César Franck, Camille Saint-Saëns, Jules Massenet, Gabriel Fauré and others gained popularity at this time.

Art was changing as a new generation of Impressionists began to challenge the rules, capturing the momentary and transient effects of sunlight and overall visual effect of colour vibration. This different way of seeing was about immediacy and movement, and the play of light expressed in a bright and varied use of colour. The sensation of the eye that views the subject in the moment was more important than the details of the subject.

A favourite meeting place for these artists was the Café Guerbois on Avenue de Clichy in Paris, where discussions were often led by **Édouard Manet**[5] (1832-1883), whom the younger artists greatly admired. Manet had grown to dislike the dominant Salon style of painting and was inspired to paint the realities of contemporary life that he saw around him, depicting the real and the mundane on a large scale.

In 1859 he painted *Le Buveur d'absinthe* (The Absinthe Drinker), one of the earliest depictions of absinthe in art (along with Honoré Daumier's Smoker with Absinth Drinker). The subject is a man named Collardet who was a rag'n'bone man and an alcoholic, known to frequent the area around the Louvre in Paris. Manet continued to revise the painting, and the glass of absinthe was added later sometime between 1867 and 1872.

---

[5] *Fried, Michael (1996). Manet's Modernism: Or, The Face of Painting in the 1860s. University of Chicago Press. p. 34. ISBN 978-0226262178.*

The Absinthe Drinker was rejected by the Paris Salon, and criticised by some as being degenerate and an abomination, notably Manet's former teacher Thomas Couture.

Among the conservative art world, the idea that a person of such low station and questionable moral fibre as an alcoholic should be presented on such a grand scale would have been abhorrent to them. In their eyes absinthe had come to symbolise the alcoholism and moral degeneracy of the lower classes.

The term Alcoholism was first used by the Swedish physician Magnus Huss in an 1852 publication to describe the systemic effects of alcohol.

The misuse of alcohol is as old as alcohol itself. What made absinthe unique however was that it allowed (or trusted) the consumer to decide by how much it was diluted for taste and strength, if at all. It was therefore easier to misuse to excess.

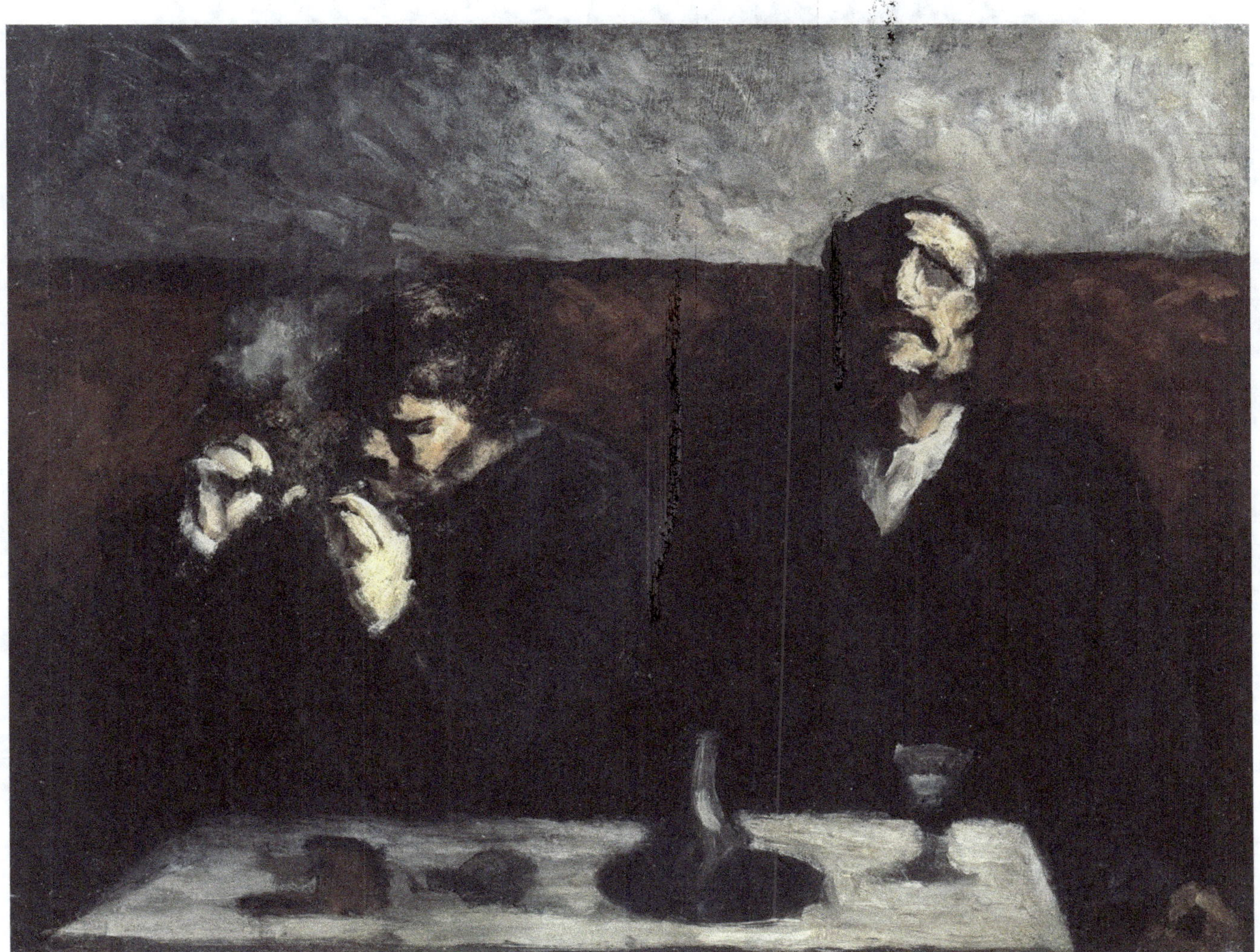

Honoré Daumier - Smoker and Absinth Drinker, c1856-1860

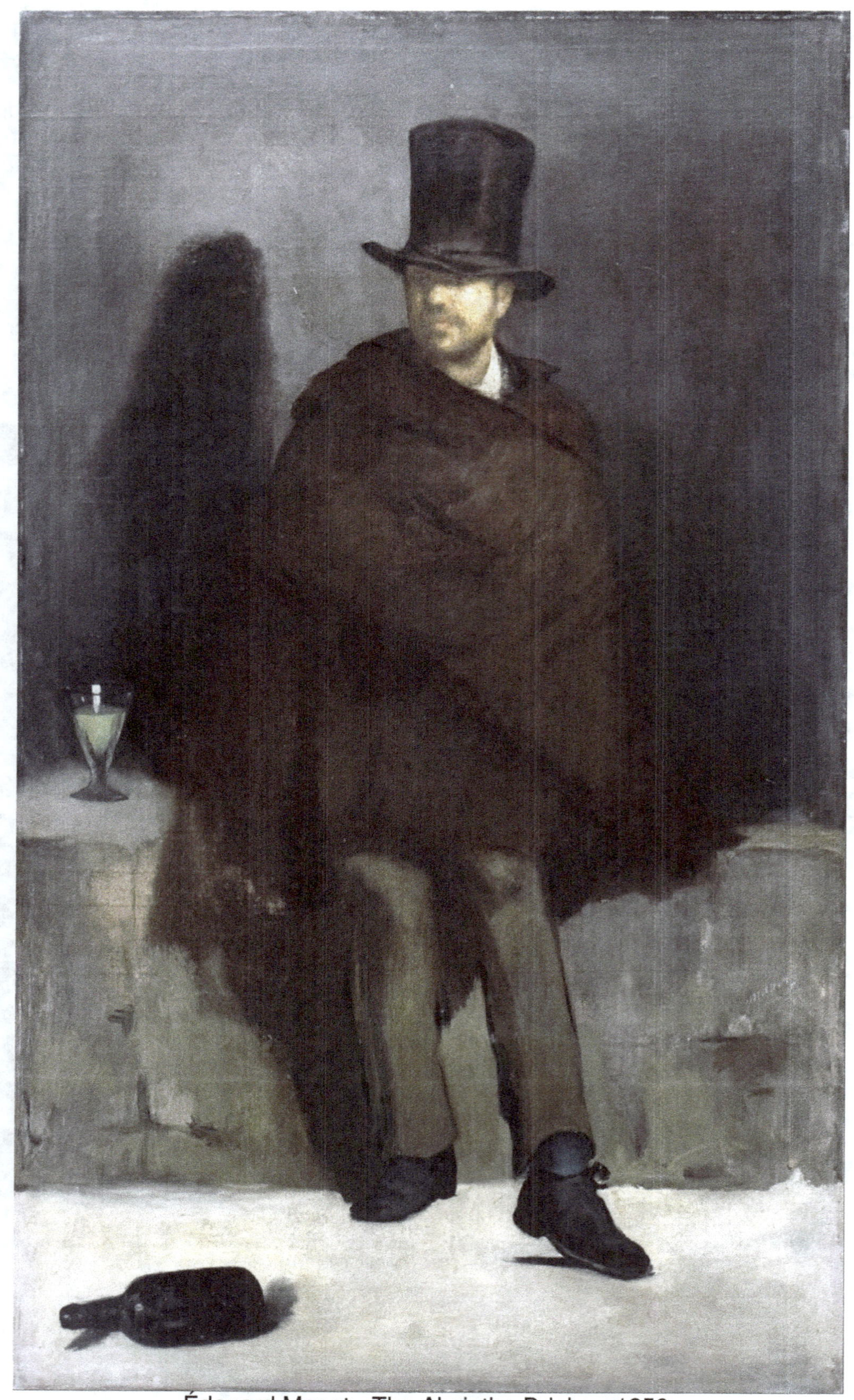

Édouard Manet - The Absinthe Drinker, 1859

5. *La Belle Époque*: The Beautiful Age

"Viens, les vins vont aux plages,
Et les flots par millions!
Vois le Bitter sauvage
Rouler du haut des monts!

Gagnons, pèlerins sages,
L'absinthe aux verts piliers..."

"Come, the wines go to the beaches,
And the waves by the millions!
See the wild Bitter
Ride from the top of the mountains!

Let us win, wise pilgrims,
Absinthe with green pillars..."

Arthur Rimbaud
Comédie de la Soif
Le recueil Derniers vers, 1872

The End of the Franco-Prussian War

France's confident position as a dominant political power in Europe at this time was increasingly challenged by the expanding North German Confederation.

The Franco-Prussian war of 1870 resulted in a victory for German Unification, the declaration of the German Empire, and the annexation of Alsace-Lorraine (in modern day France).

For France it resulted in the capture and abdication of Napoleon III, the end of the Second Empire, and the creation of the Third Republic.

The peace and relative stability of the following period, as experienced by some, gave birth to a sense of optimism, affluence, economic prosperity, colonial expansion, and technological, scientific, and cultural innovations.

After the horrors of World War 1, this period became known retrospectively and nostalgically across continental Europe as *La Belle Époque* (The Beautiful Age). This corresponded with the second half of the Victorian Era in Britain, and The Gilded Age in the United States.

Absinthe Exports

Absinthe from France and Switzerland was exported widely and gained some popularity in the United States (also in Spain, the United Kingdom, and Czechoslovakia).

New Orleans has an association with absinthe culture and is credited with being the birthplace of the Sazerac cocktail[6], perhaps the first absinthe cocktail, consisting of 50 ml cognac, 10 ml absinthe, one sugar cube, and two dashes Peychaud's Bitters. The IBA (International Bartenders Association) describes its preparation thus:

> *"Rinse a chilled old-fashioned glass with the absinthe, add crushed ice and set it aside. Stir the remaining ingredients over ice in a mixing glass. Discard the ice and any excess absinthe from the prepared glass, strain the mixed drink into the glass."..."Garnish with lemon zest".*

The original recipe changed after the American Civil War when Rye Whiskey substituted Cognac as it became hard to obtain. The Old Absinthe House bar on Bourbon Street began selling absinthe in the

---

[6] *Simon, Kate (2010). Absinthe Cocktails: 50 Ways to Mix with the Green Fairy. Chronicle Books. p. 33. ISBN 978-1452100302.*

first half of the 19th century. The lease-holder Cayetano Ferrer named it The Absinthe Room in 1874 due to the popularity of the drink which was served in the Parisian style.

The Arts

Often when there is a period of relative stability in history, the arts flourish. In France, those who did experience the prosperity of the age enjoyed new forms of entertainment in music halls, cabarets, and bistros such as the Casino de Paris, Moulin Rouge, Folies Bergère, and Le Chat Noir.

In European cities, new generations of artists, writers, poets, journalists, intellectuals, musicians, and performers were living Bohemian lifestyles away from society's conventions and expectations. Their innovations and masterpieces of literature, music, theatre, and visual art gained wide recognition around the world.

Avec les fleurs, avec les femmes,	With flowers, with women,
Avec l'absinthe, avec le feu,	With wormwood, with fire,
On peut se divertir un peu,	We can have a little fun,
Jouer son rôle en quelque drame.	Play your role in some drama.
L'absinthe bue un soir d'hiver	Absinthe drunk on a winter evening
Eclaire en vert l'âme enfumée,	Lights up the smoky soul in green,
Et les fleurs, sur la bien-aimée	And the flowers, on the beloved
Embaument devant le feu clair.	Embalming in front of a bright fire.

Charles Cros
Lendemain
Le Coffret de santal, 1873

Another popular café for artists was the Café de la Nouvelle-Athènes on Rue Pigalle, Paris. The composer **Erik Satie** played piano there. The Impressionists discussed art and planned their first exhibition there, and **Edgar Degas**[7] (1834-1917) used it for the location of his piece called *Dans un Café*. The painting depicts a man and a woman sitting side by side, drinking a glass of absinthe. It was first shown in 1876 where it was met with very negative criticism. It was put in storage until it resurfaced again in 1892, but was again heavily criticised. In 1893 it was shown in London where it became known as *L'Absinthe* or The Absinthe Drinker.

In London it caused even greater controversy. It was described by English critics as shockingly degraded and uncouth. Some regarded it as an indictment of morality and a warning about absinthe and the decadence of French culture in general. Such a reaction was typical of the outward high-mindedness of the age, and also the mistrust with which Victorian England viewed French art, as dangerous or subversive.

Artists became inspired by the growing absinthe culture that they saw around them, experienced, and embraced. They created art that went against the traditional rules. Instead of crystal clear allegories of biblical or mythological narrative events intended to be morally uplifting, showing the way the world *ought* to be, they painted the world as it really *was*.

To the modern audience, rather than inducing moral panic, *L'Absinthe* depicts a moment frozen in time of two people, who while enjoying a glass of absinthe, enter a *reverie*, taking a moment to become pleasantly lost in their own thoughts. We wonder what they are thinking about, and about what their lives are like, and what it must have been like to be in such a place at such a time.

---

[7] Siegel, Ronald K. (2005). *Intoxication: The Universal Drive for Mind-Altering Substances. Inner Traditions / Bear & Co.* ISBN 978-1594770692.

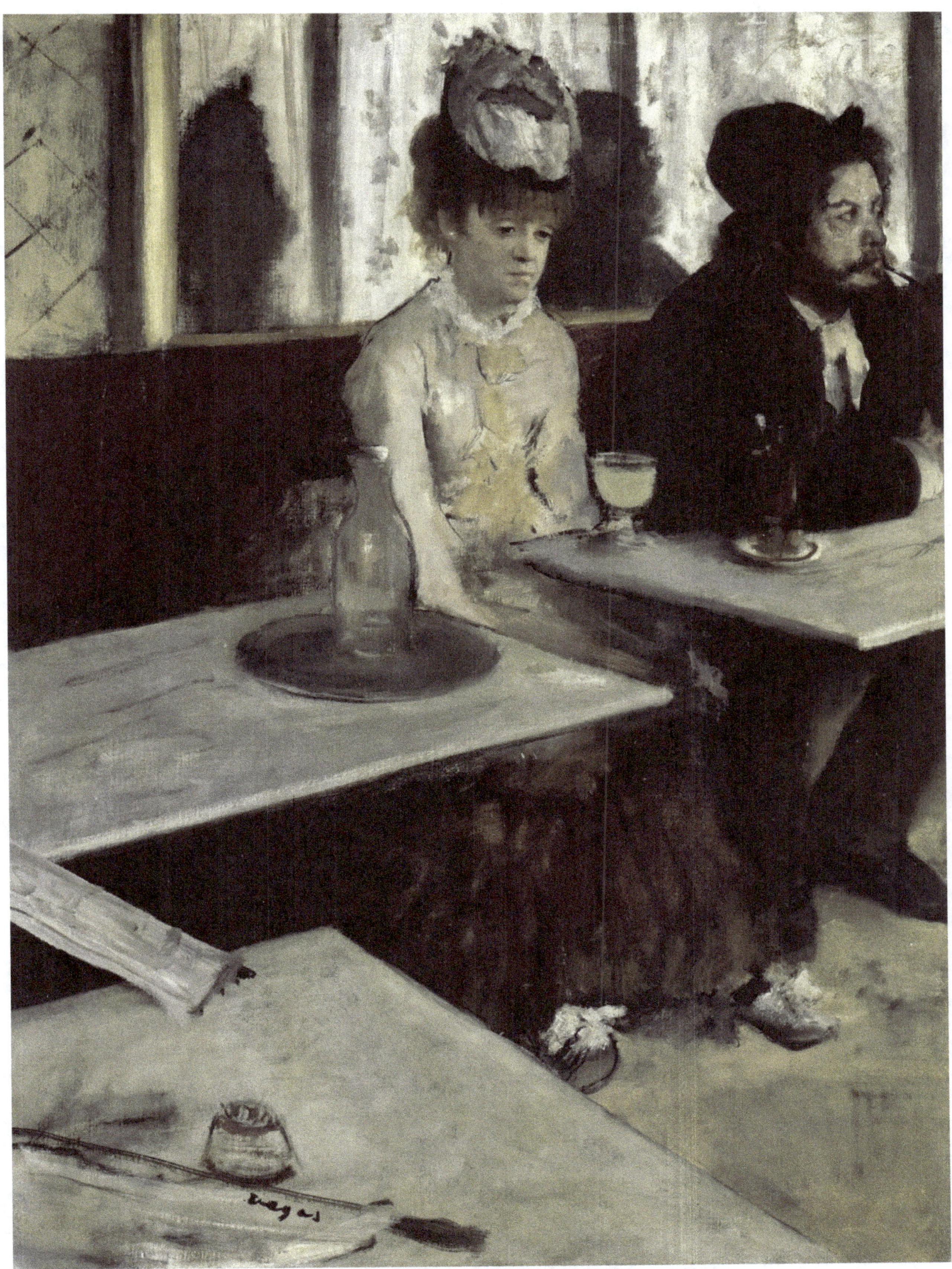

Edgar Degas - L'Absinthe, 1876

"Comme bercée en un hamac
La pensée oscille et tournoie,
A cette heure où tout estomac
Dans un flot d'absinthe se noie.

Et l'absinthe pénètre l'air,
Car cette heure est toute émeraude.
L'appétit aiguise le flair
De plus d'un nez rose qui rode"

"As cradled in a hammock,
Thought sways and twirls,
At this time when every stomach
In a flood of absinthe drowns.

And absinthe penetrates the air,
Because this hour is all emerald.
Appetite sharpens the flair
Plus a prowling pink nose"

Charles Cros
L'Heure Verte
Le Coffret de Santal, 1873

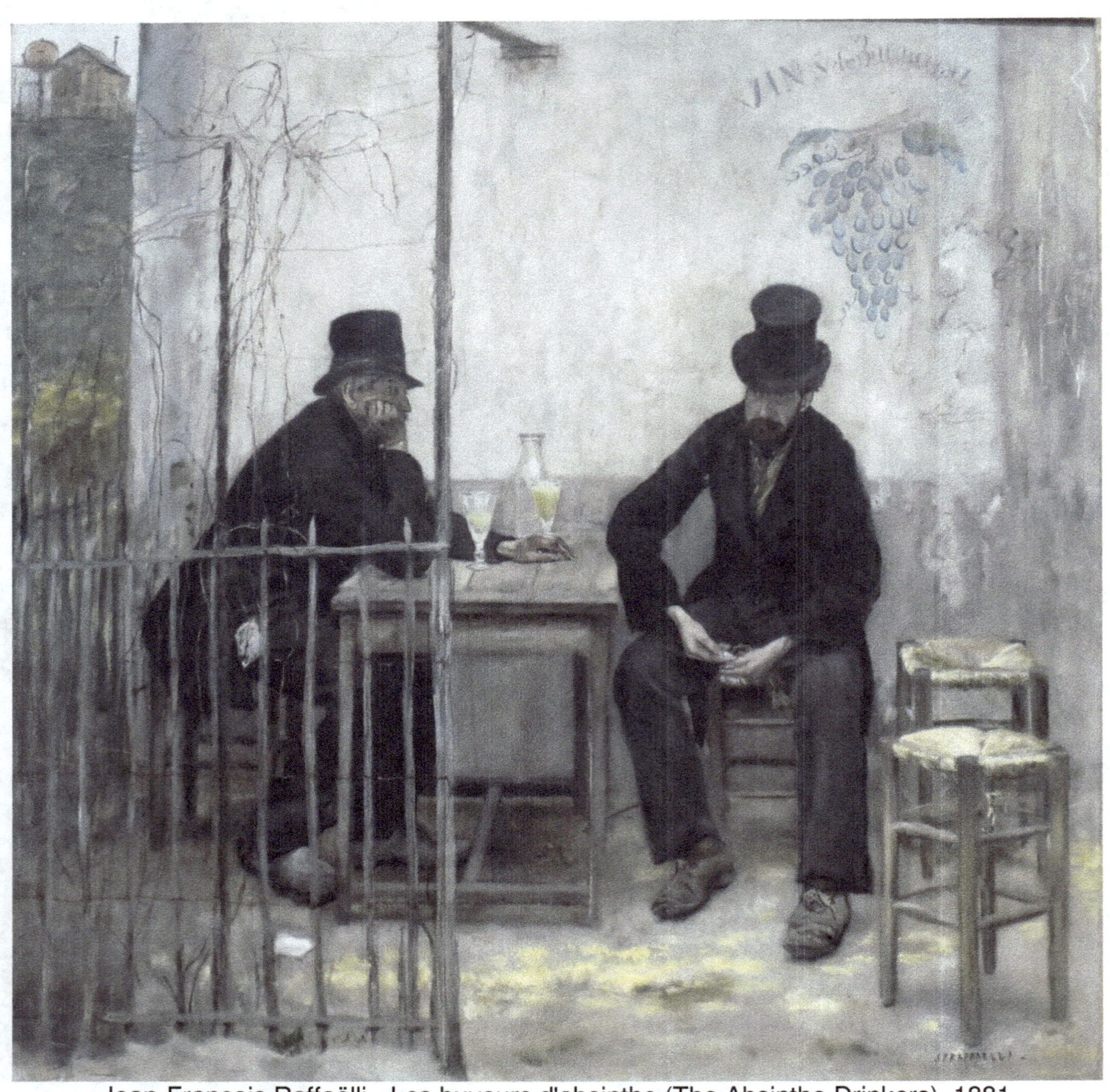

Jean-François Raffaëlli - Les buveurs d'absinthe (The Absinthe Drinkers), 1881

> "A glass of absinthe is as poetical as anything in the world. What difference
> is there between a glass of absinthe and a sunset?"

Oscar Wilde, while touring America, 1882

Henri de Toulouse-Lautrec[8] (1864-1901) was a prolific painter, printmaker, draughtsman, caricaturist, and illustrator. He was immersed in the colourful and theatrical life of Paris, producing posters for various shows which visually contributed to the spirit of the age.

Due to his short stature, disability, and health problems, he walked with the aid of a cane, which he hollowed out in order to fit a thin flask of absinthe and a small glass.

He was also fascinated by the lives of the urban underclass, and as someone who frequented brothels, he produced many sketches and paintings of prostitutes, and was uniquely placed to capture and reflect the decadent affairs of the nightlife of the time.

Born into French aristocracy, he had a regular income from his family. When the Moulin Rouge cabaret opened in 1889, Toulouse-Lautrec was commissioned to produce a series of posters, which gave him the opportunity to make a living of his own. The cabaret reserved a seat for him and displayed his paintings of famous singers and dancers of the day.

The symbolist painter Gustave Moreau commented that Toulouse-Lautrec's paintings "are entirely painted in absinthe". Toulouse-Lautrec himself commented: "To me, in the colour green, there is something like the temptation of the devil".

While attending the open studio of Fernand Cormon in Paris from 1886 to 1887 Toulouse-Lautrec met **Vincent Van Gogh** (1853-1890). Van Gogh had moved to Paris in March 1886 to live with his brother Theo in Montmartre.

One evening in 1887 at the Café du Tambourin on the Boulevard de Clichy, Toulouse-Lautrec created a chalk pastel portrait on cardboard of Van Gogh, in profile from the right, leaning forward at a table, with a glass of absinthe, perhaps as if in conversation with an unknown figure out of the picture to the right. It is a brightly coloured Impressionist work, rich in light blues and hints of green. It arguably captures something of an absinthe-like glow or haze around Van Gogh. Toulouse-Lautrec used a similarly impressionistic style in his work Monsieur Boileau of 1893.

The Café du Tambourin's proprietor was Agostina Segatori, with whom Van Gogh was rumoured to be having a love affair with. As an artist's model, he had painted her at least twice. They had an arrangement whereby Van Gogh would give his artworks to Segatori when he was unable to pay his bills.

That same year Van Gogh produced a still life simply titled Glass of Absinthe and a Carafe. It depicts a table in a café with a view of the street in the background. On the table is a carafe and a glass of absinthe.

The sunlight enters the windows and plays upon the carafe and the glass of absinthe, reflecting light in various directions. The light colours in the foreground contrast with the brown colours of the wooden café interior in the background.

---

[8] *Wittels, Betina; Hermesch, Robert (2008). Absinthe, Sip of Seduction: A Contemporary Guide. Fulcrum Publishing. ISBN 978-1933108216.*

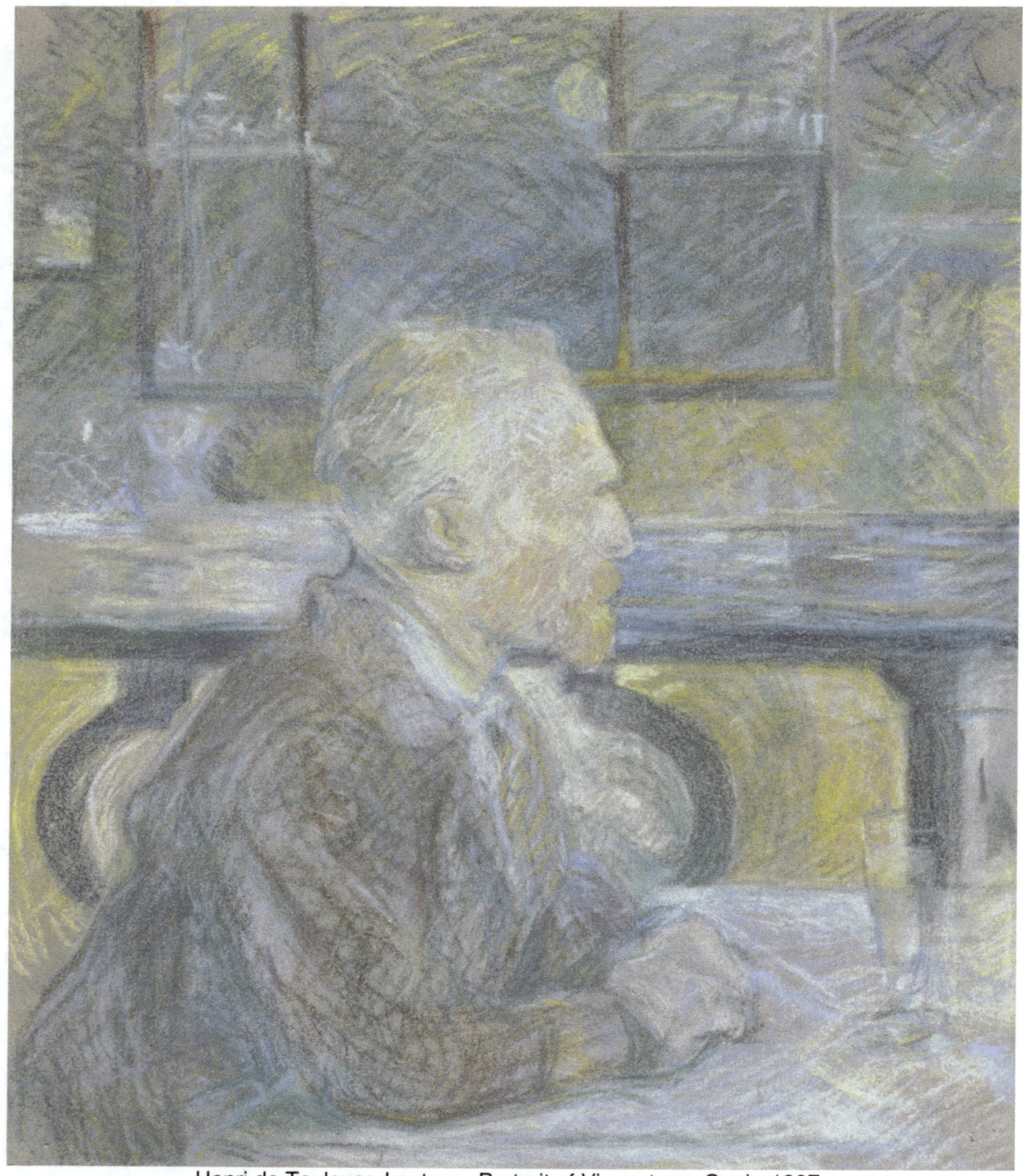

Henri de Toulouse-Lautrec - Portrait of Vincent van Gogh, 1887

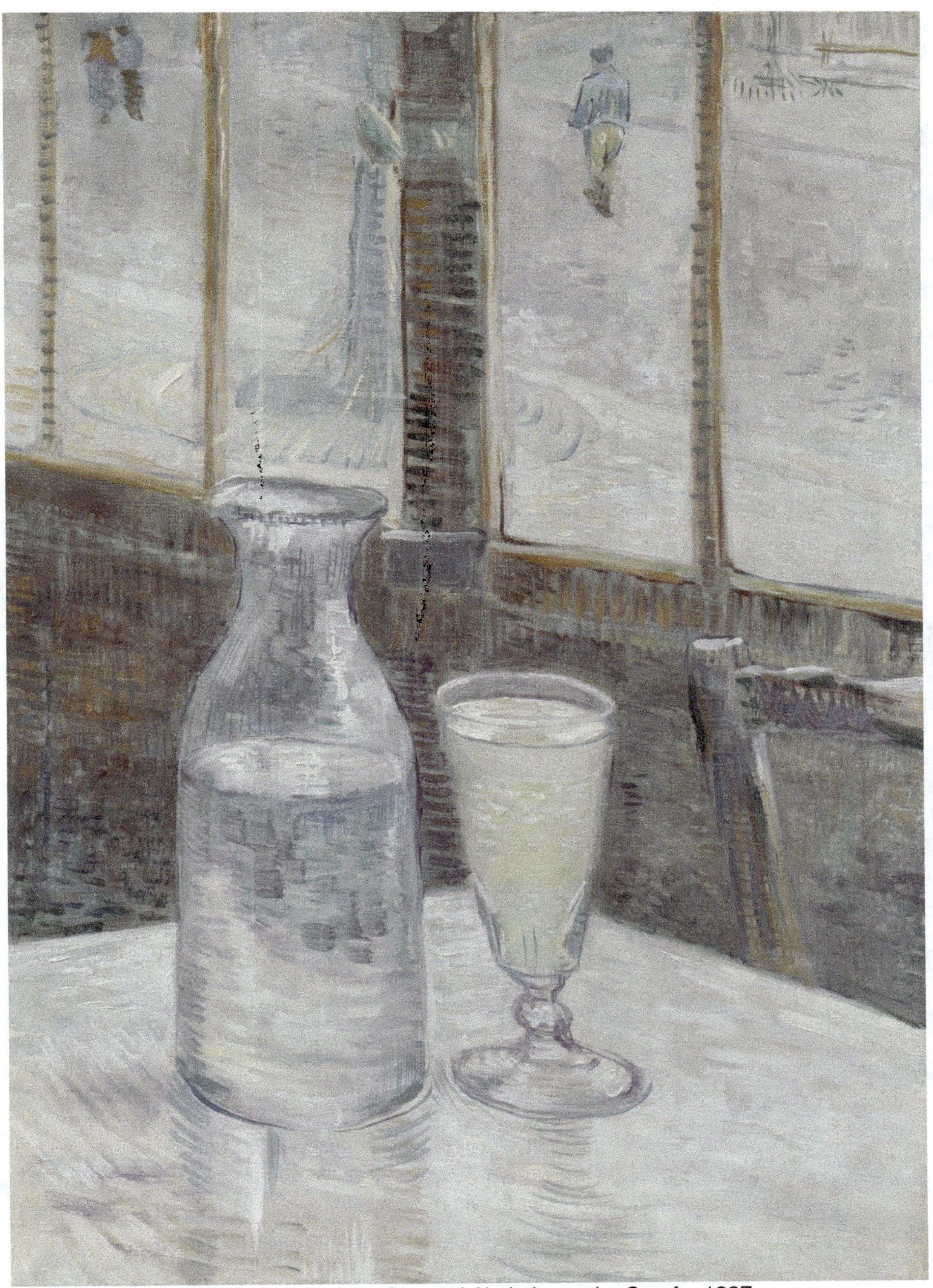

Vincent Van Gogh - Glass of Absinthe and a Carafe, 1887

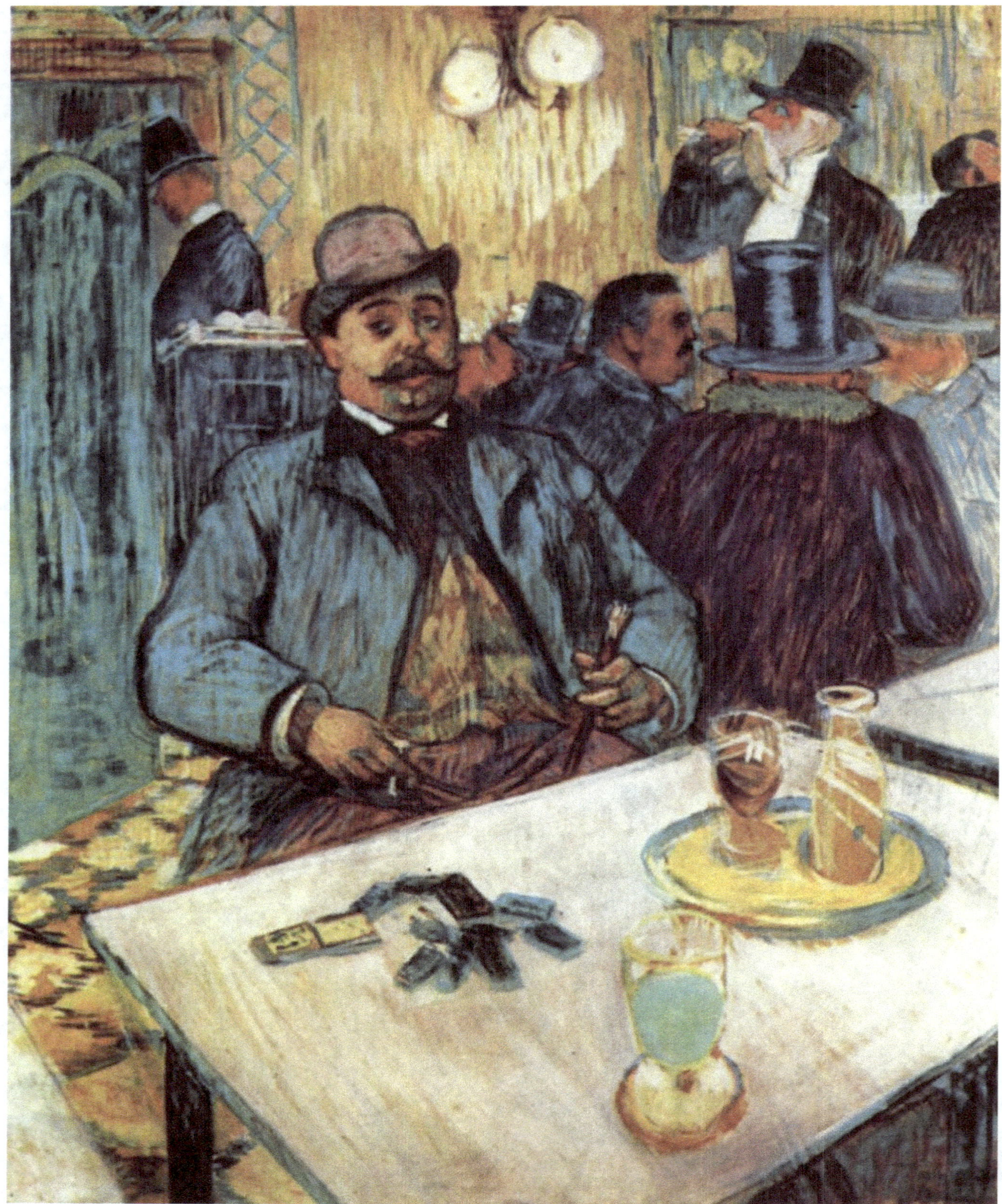

Henri de Toulouse-Lautrec - Monsieur Boileau, 1893

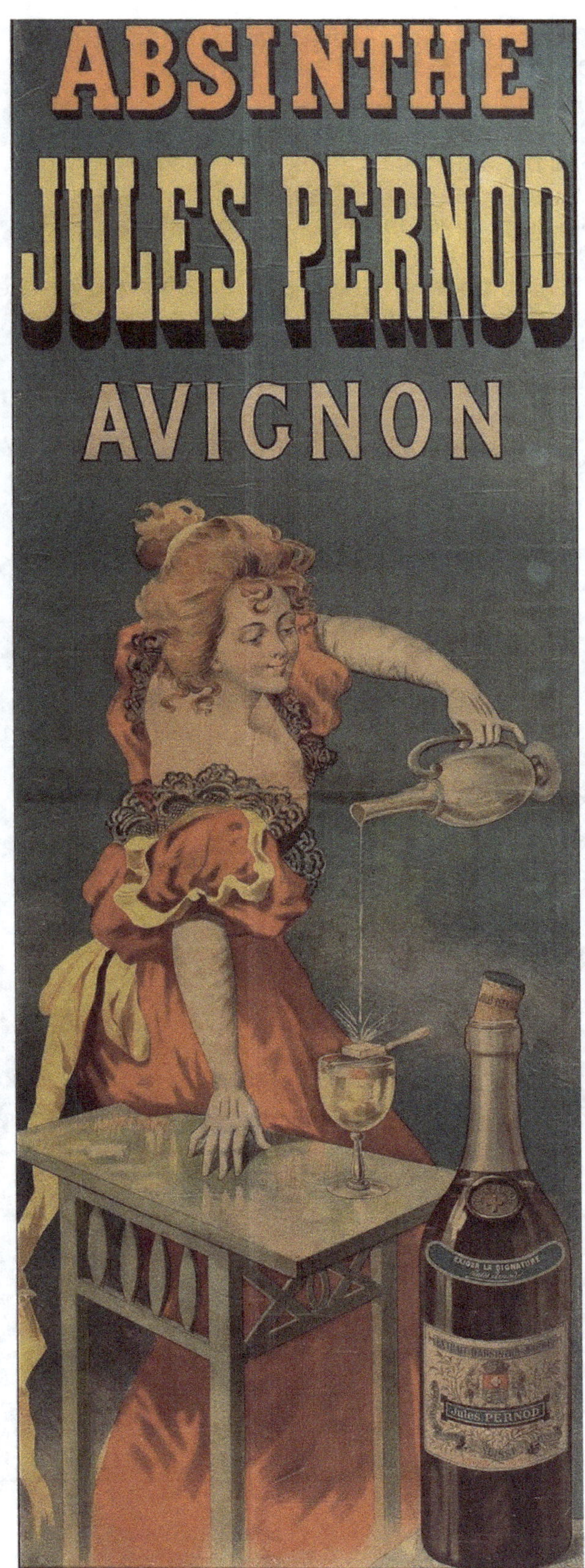

Absinthe Jules Pernod Avignon, 1888

Paul Verlaine[9] (1844-1896) was a French poet associated with the Symbolist movement (absolute truths expressed symbolically) and the Decadent movement (an aesthetic ideology of excess and artificiality). He is considered one of the greatest representatives of the *fin de siècle* (end of the century) in poetry.

In 1871 he received a letter from Arthur Rimbaud praising his poetry, and including a few of his own poems. Verlaine was intrigued and invited Rimbaud to join him in Paris.

They soon became lovers and engaged in an affair, leading a wild and drifting lifestyle with frequent use of absinthe, opium, and hashish. Their stormy relationship soon turned sour however, and Verlaine abandoned Rimbaud in London.

Their reunion at the Grand Hôtel Liégeois in Brussels in the summer of 1873 went badly, and in a drunken rage, Verlaine fired two shots at Rimbaud, one of which wounded him in the left wrist. Verlaine was later arrested and sentenced to two years in prison.

In 1874, while Verlaine was in prison, a collection of his poems was published under the title *Romances sans paroles* (Romances without words).

The poems on the one hand looked back nostalgically at his life with Mathilde, and on the other hand made impressionistic sketches of his turbulent affair with Rimbaud.

As Verlaine descended into drug addiction, alcoholism, and poverty, he spent his days drinking absinthe in Paris cafés. His early poetry was later rediscovered and celebrated as groundbreaking, most notably his 1869 poem *Clair de lune* (moonlight).

Of particular inspiration to musicians and composers, it was set to music by Gabriel Fauré, Louis Vierne, Sigfrid Karg-Elert, Josef Szulc, Alphons Diepenbrock, and most famously by Claude Debussy, in the third movement of his *Suite Bergamasque* in 1890.

---

[9] *Phillips, Rod (2014-10-13). Alcohol: A History. UNC Press Books. p. 180. ISBN 978-1469617619.*

Votre âme est un paysage choisi *Que vont charmant masques et bergamasques* *Jouant du luth et dansant et quasi* *Tristes sous leurs déguisements fantasques.*	Your soul is a chosen landscape On which masks and Bergamasques cast enchantment as they go, Playing the lute, and dancing, and all but Sad beneath their fantasy-disguises.
Tout en chantant sur le mode mineur *L'amour vainqueur et la vie opportune* *Ils n'ont pas l'air de croire à leur bonheur* *Et leur chanson se mêle au clair de lune,*	Singing all the while, in the minor mode, Of all-conquering love and life so kind to them They do not seem to believe in their good fortune, And their song mingles with the moonlight,
Au calme clair de lune triste et beau, *Qui fait rêver les oiseaux dans les arbres* *Et sangloter d'extase les jets d'eau,* *Les grands jets d'eau sveltes parmi les marbres.*	With the calm moonlight, sad and lovely, Which makes the birds dream in the trees, And the plumes of the fountains weep in ecstasy, The tall, slender plumes of the fountains among the marble sculptures.

Paul Verlaine, Claire de lune, 1869

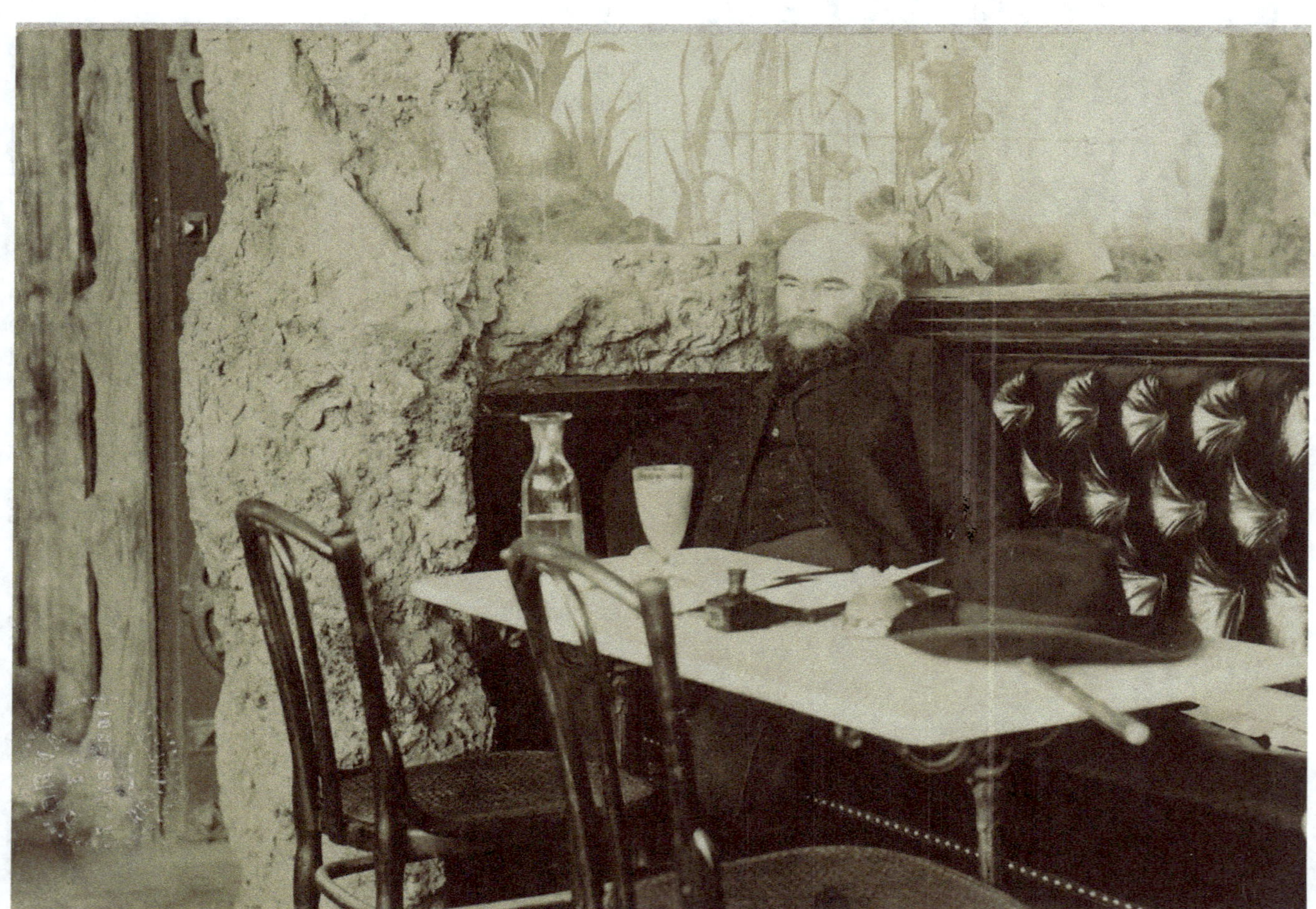

Paul Verlaine drinking absinthe in the Café François 1er in 1892 by Dornac

Art Nouveau

In the last decade of the 19th century, a style of art emerged that would be referred to as Art Nouveau (New Art). Inspired by the curves of plants and nature, it contained dynamism, movement, and asymmetry.

In architecture and interior design, it made use of modern materials such as iron, glass, ceramics, and concrete to create unusual forms in open spaces. It lent itself to the German aesthetic ideal of *Gesamtkunstwerk* (Total Artwork) of unifying architecture, furnishings, and interior art in a common style that would be uplifting for residents.

Originating in Brussels, Art Nouveau was quickly adopted in Paris, and across the rest of Europe. The Architect Victor Horta applied the style to the Hôtel Tassel, which was completed in 1893, and in 1900, Hector Guimard applied it to the entrances of the new Paris Métro.

It was also widely used in the graphic arts, particularly in commercial art and posters. Many of these posters have since appeared in exhibitions relating to both Art Nouveau and La Belle Époque. Their enduring appeal is demonstrated to this day by their availability as prints on canvases and metal signs, and as decoration on a wide range of household items such as trays and tins for adding a touch of Belle Époque to one's themed bar area.

Jules Chéret (1836-1932) was a French painter and lithographer who became a master of poster art, often referred to as the father of the modern poster. He created vivid poster adverts for the cabarets, music halls, and theatres such as the Eldorado, the Olympia, the Folies Bergère, Théâtre de l'Opéra, the Alcazar d'Été and the Moulin Rouge. Sometime between 1896 and 1900 he created a poster for the Get Brothers and their peppermint liqueur simply called Pippermint. One of his best known works, it exemplified the spirit of the age. It is also worth noting that some absinthes have peppermint in their ingredients and a menthol flavour.

Albert Maingnan (1845-1908) was a French history painter and illustrator. In 1889, he won a gold medal at the Exposition Universelle and received the Medal of Honour at the Salon in 1892. Three years later, he was named a Knight in the Légion d'honneur. In 1895 Maingnan painted The Green Muse, which shows a poet being overcome by the Green Fairy.

Alphonse Mucha (1860-1939) was a Czech painter, illustrator, and graphic artist living in Paris who is widely known for his distinctive posters. He produced illustrations, advertisements, decorative panels, as well as designs, which became among the best-known images of the period.

Henri Privat-Livemont (1861-1936) was an artist born in Brussels, Belgium. From 1883 to 1889, he worked and studied in the studios of Lemaire, Lavastre & Duvignaud. With Lemaire he created the decor of the Theatre Français as well as the Hôtel de Ville, Paris. He later moved back to Brussels, and worked on theatres and casinos there. In 1897, he worked on the poster for the Brussels International Exposition of 1897.

In 1896 Privat-Livemont produced a poster for the absinthe brand Absinthe Robette. It is often mistakenly attributed to Alphonse Mucha due to its similar style. It is one of the most striking and beautiful works of art inspired by absinthe.

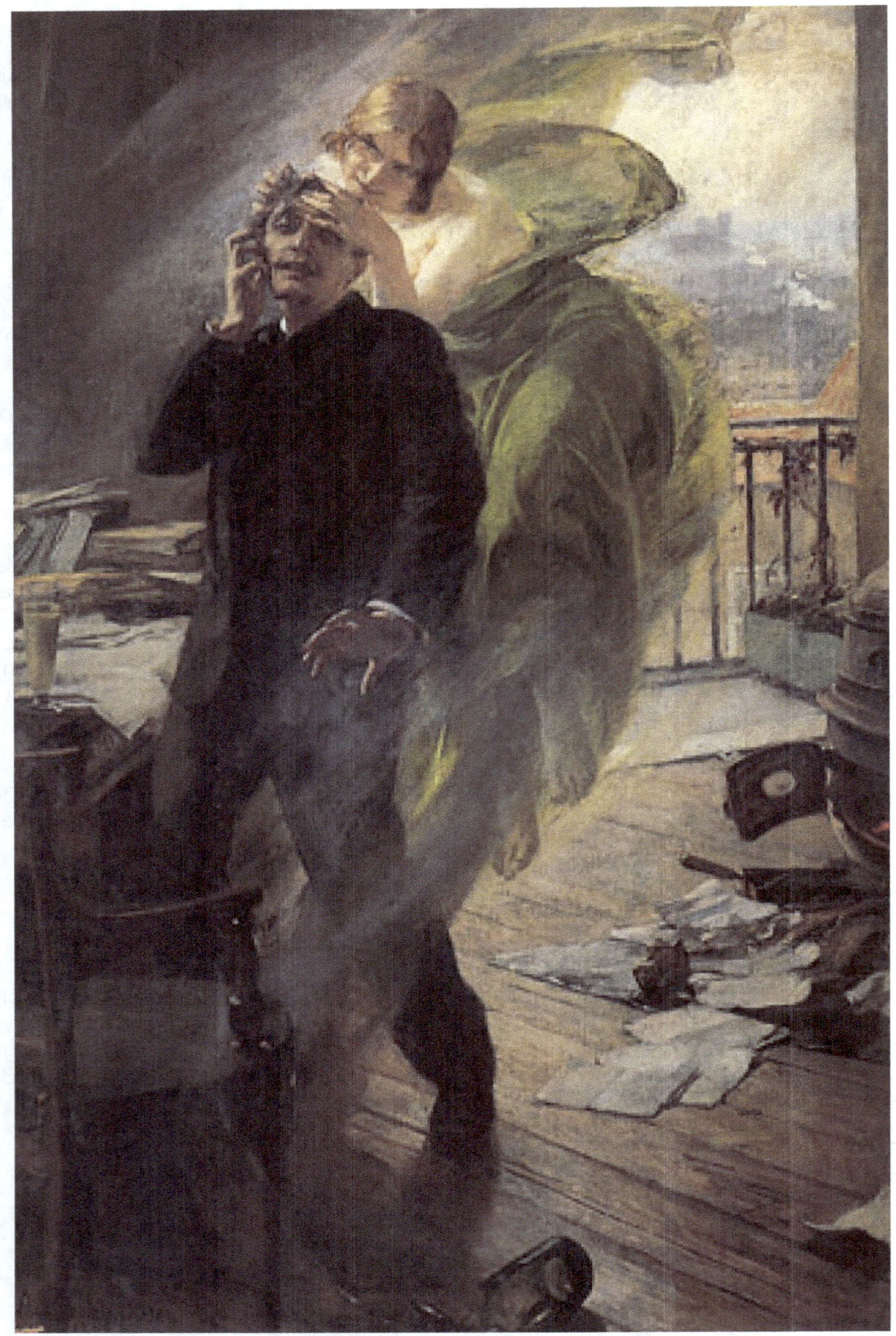

Albert Maignan - The Green Muse, 1895

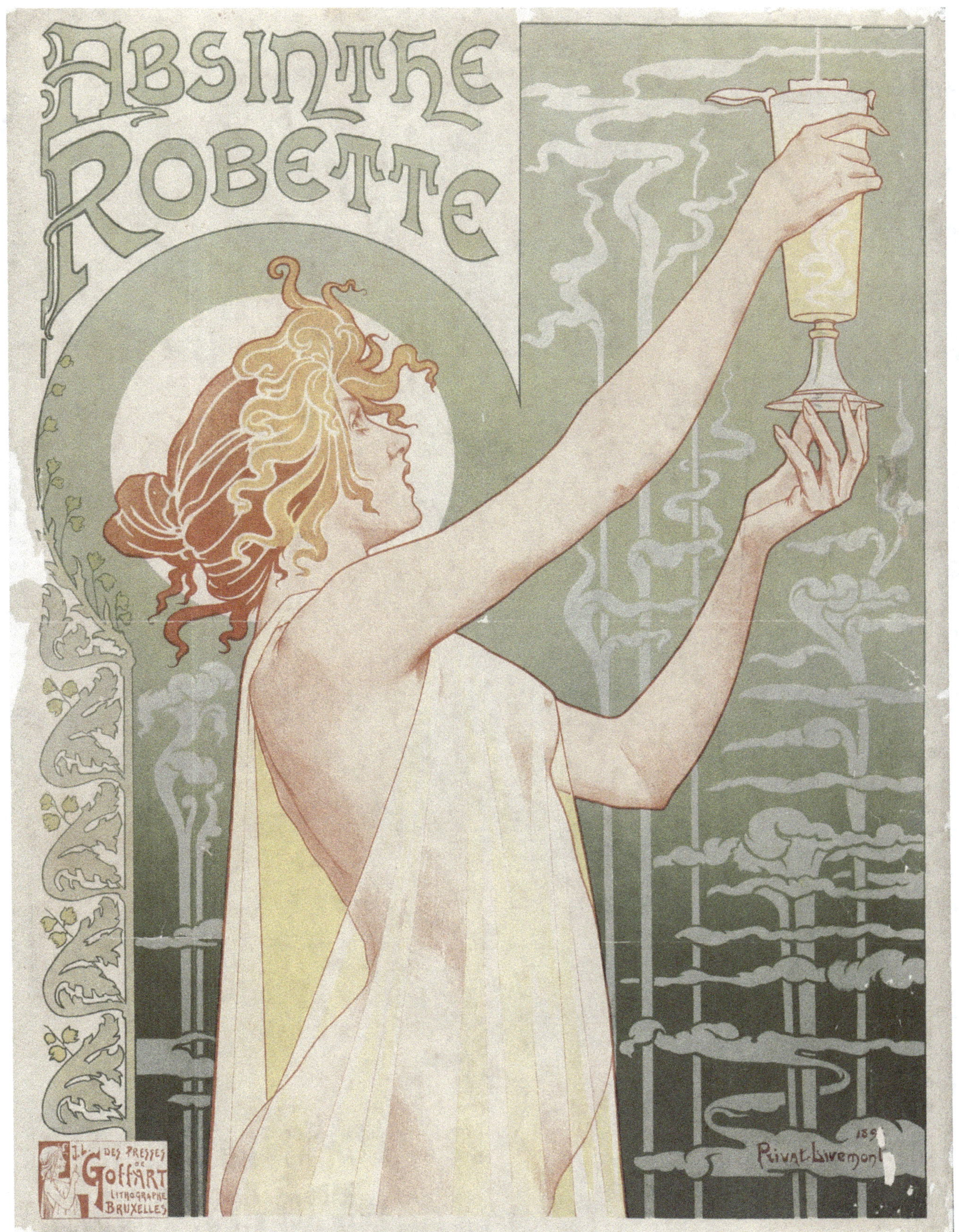

Henri Privat-Livemont - Absinthe Robinette, 1896

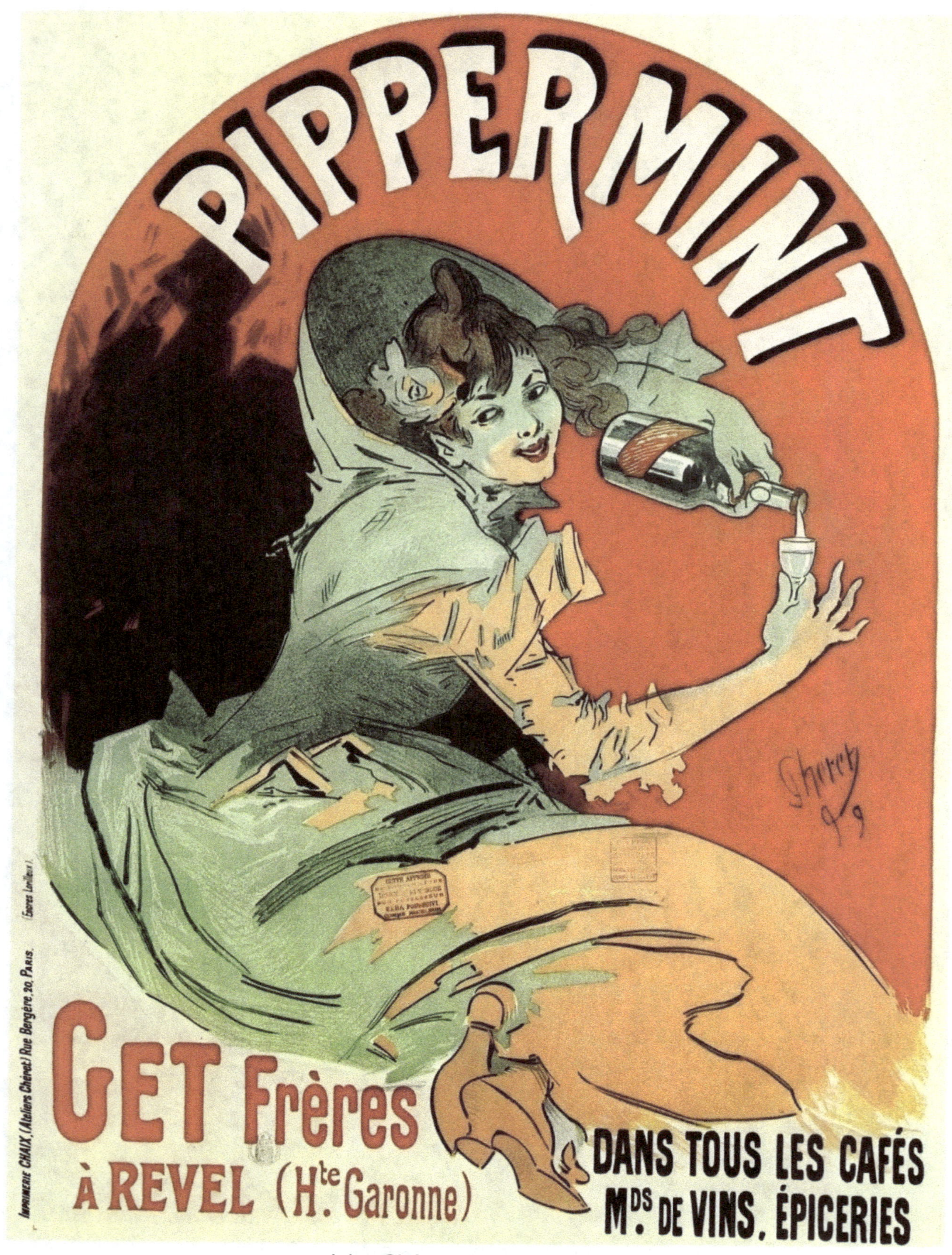

Jules Chéret - Pippermint, 1896

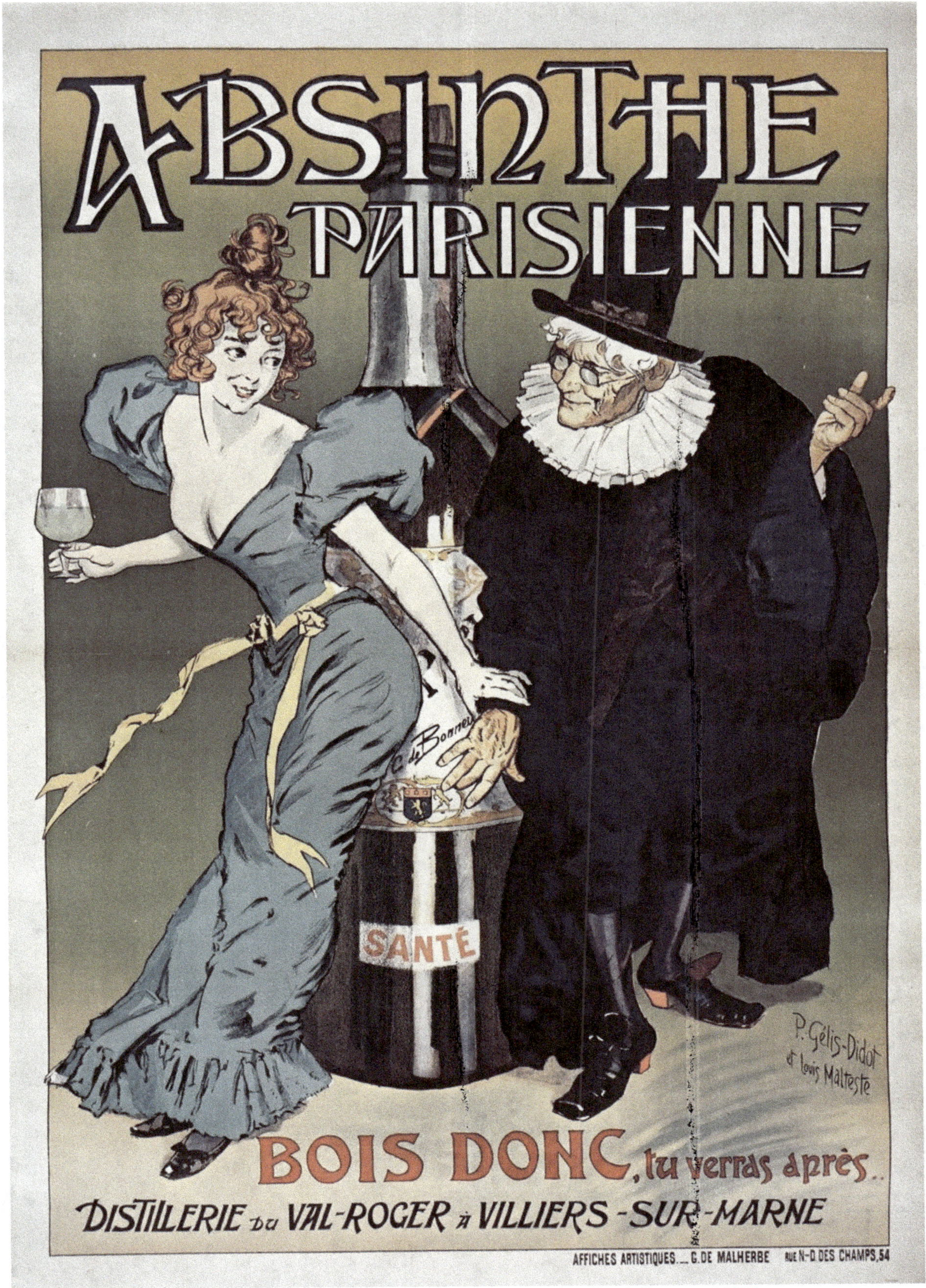

P Gélis-Didot & Louis Malteste - Absinthe Parisienne, 1896

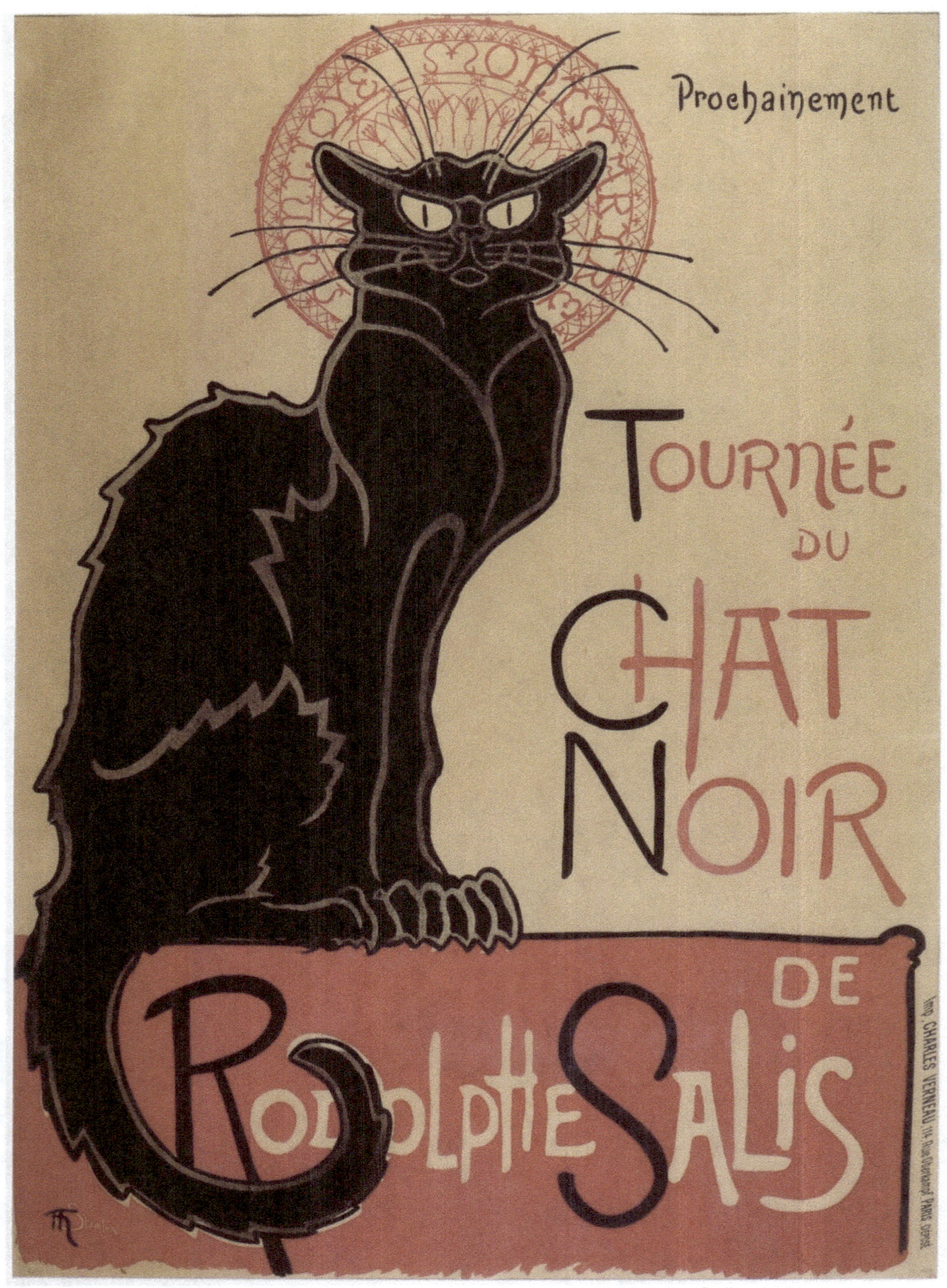

Theophile Steinlen - Tournee du Chat Noir de Rudolphe Salis, 1896

	

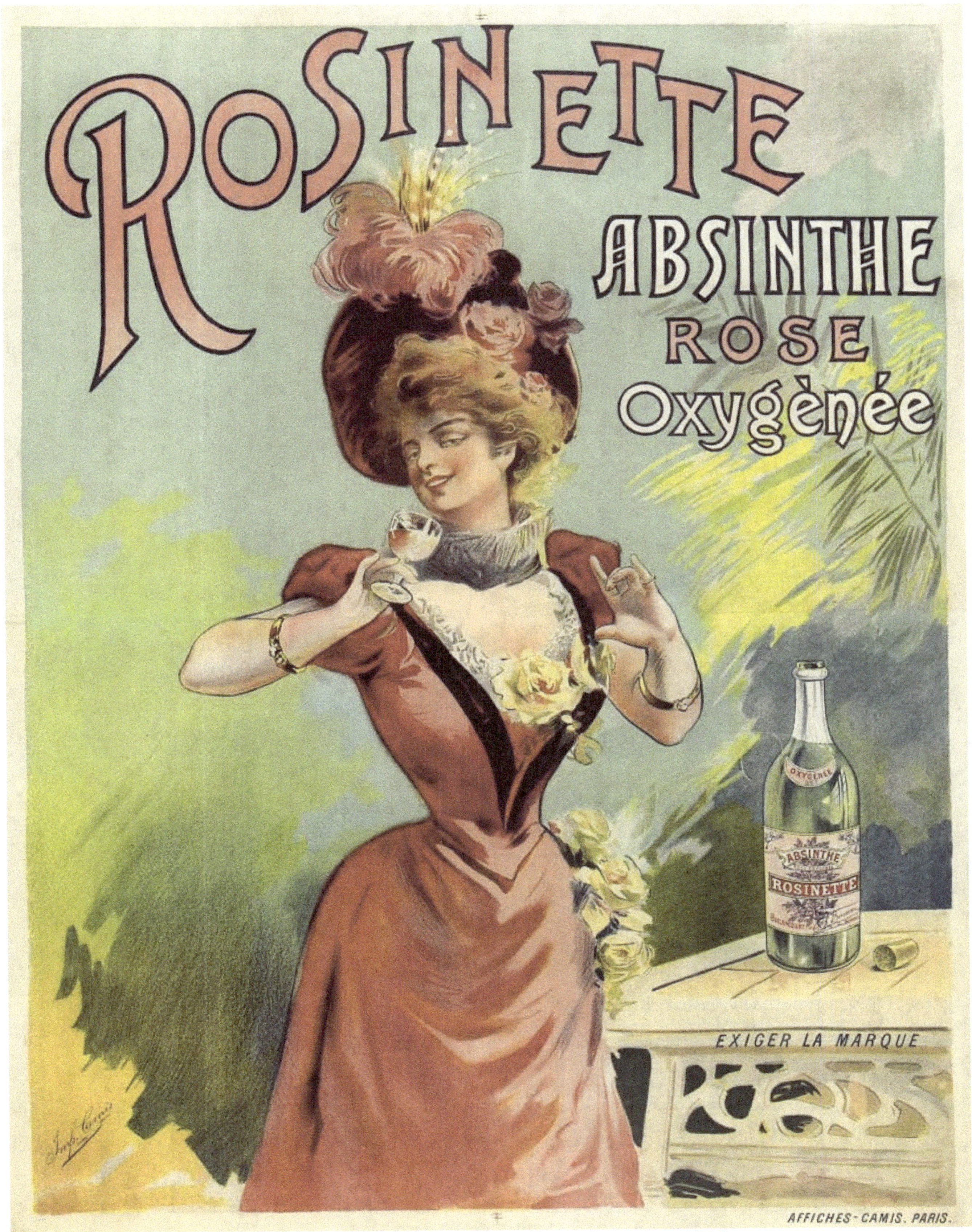

Absinthe Rosinette, Absinthe Rose Oxygene, 1900

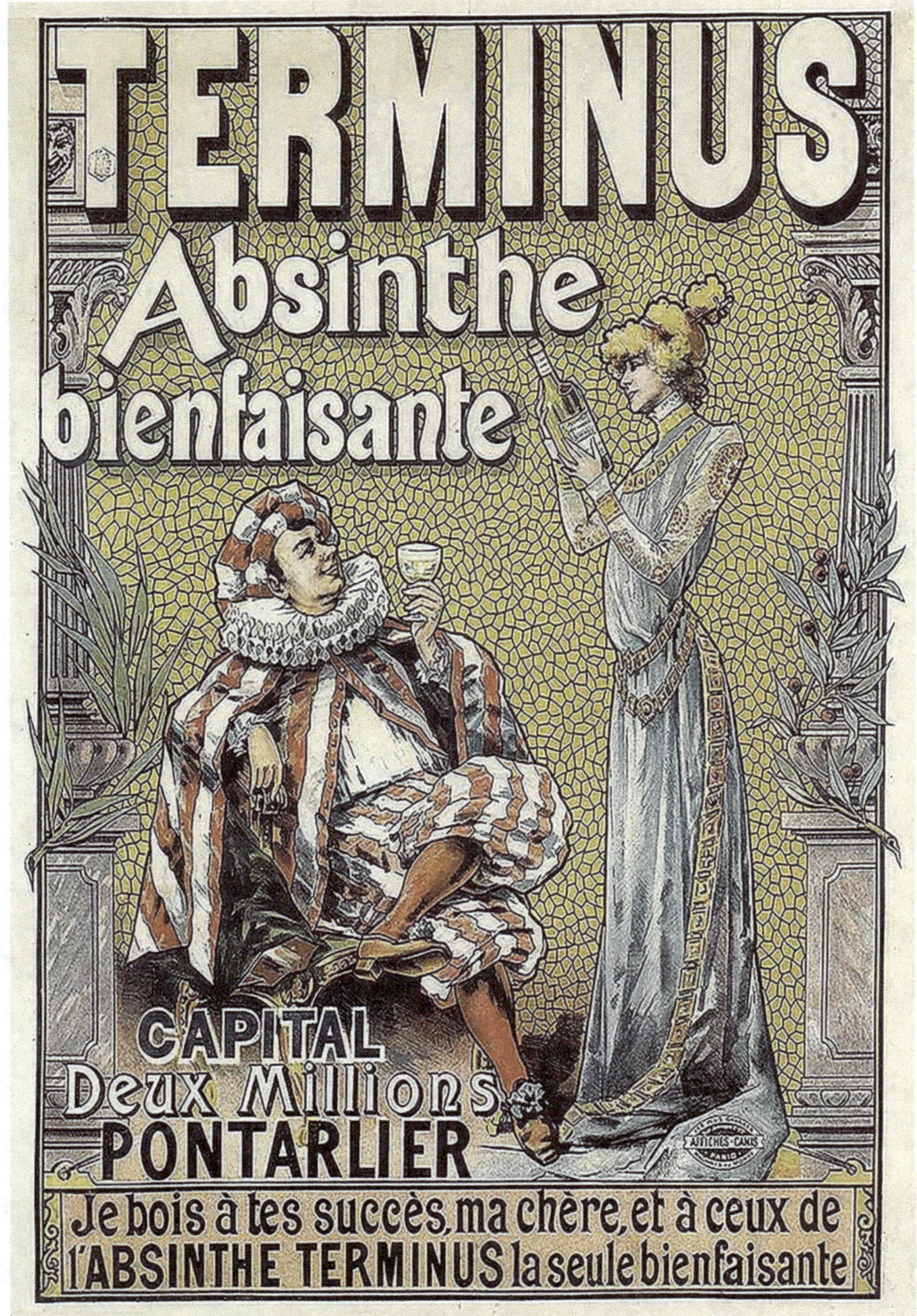

Terminus Absinthe Bienfaisante, 1890s

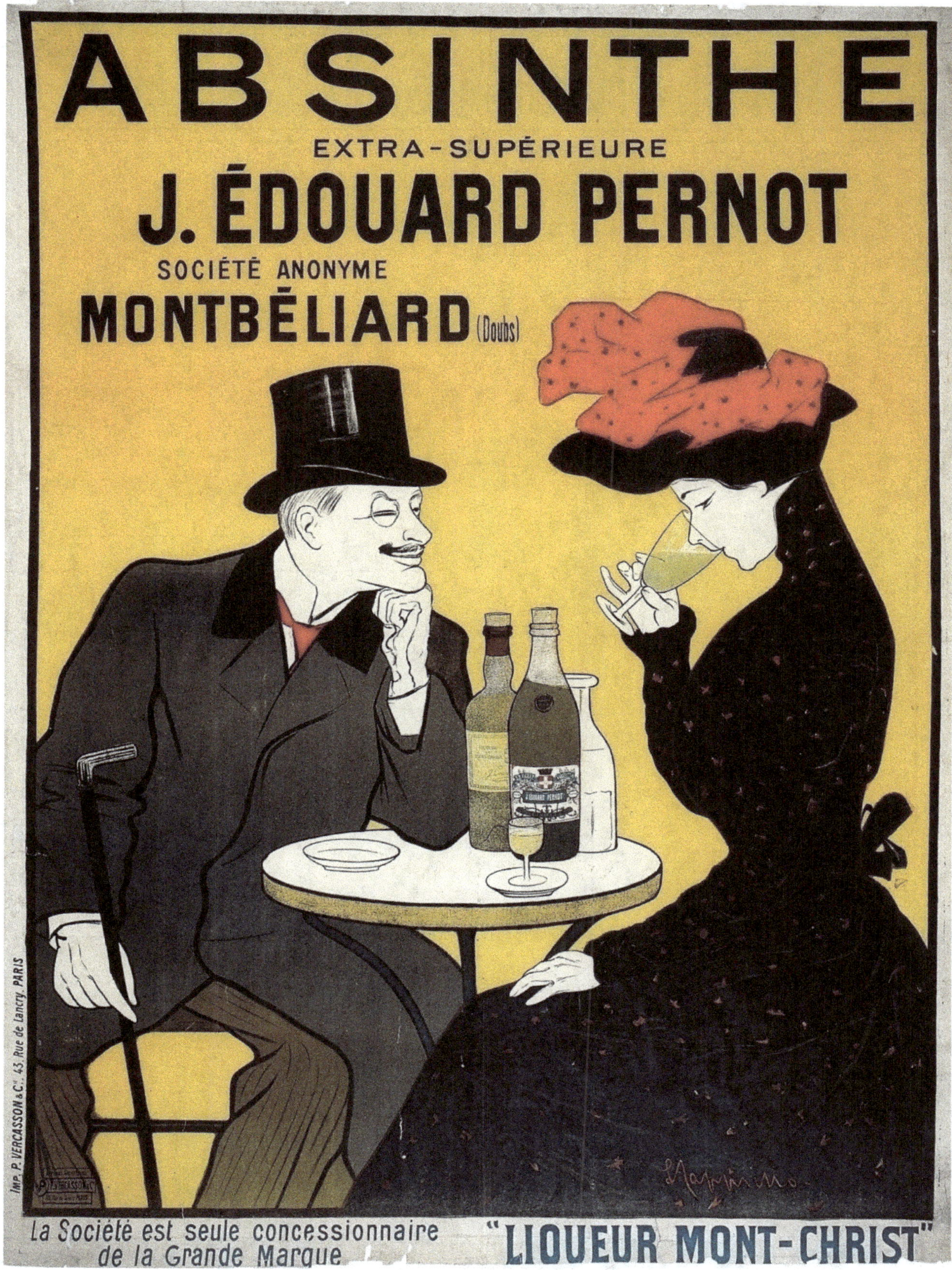

Absinthe J Edouard Pernot, c1900-1903

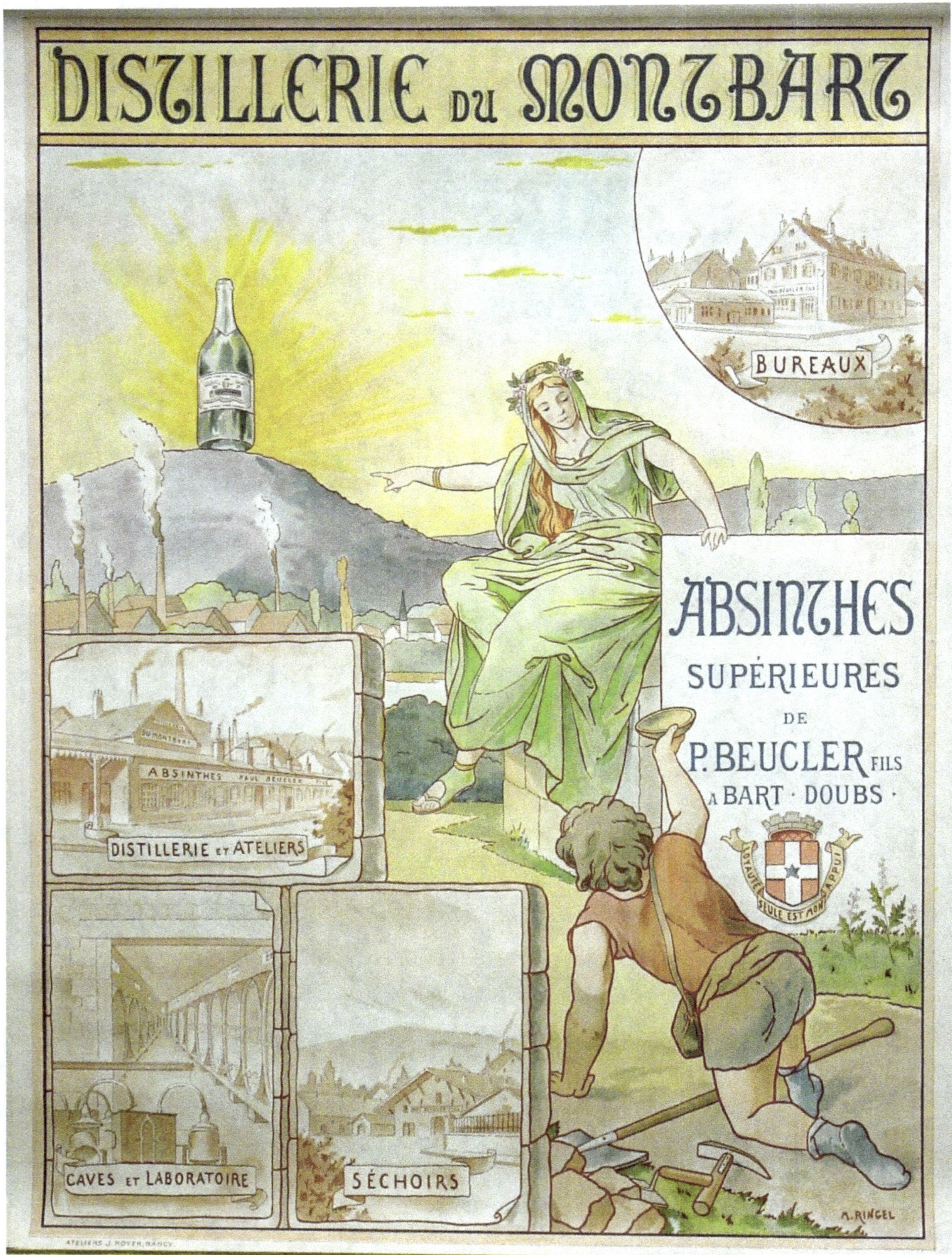

M Ringel - Absinthe Paul Beucler Distillerie du Montbart, 1900

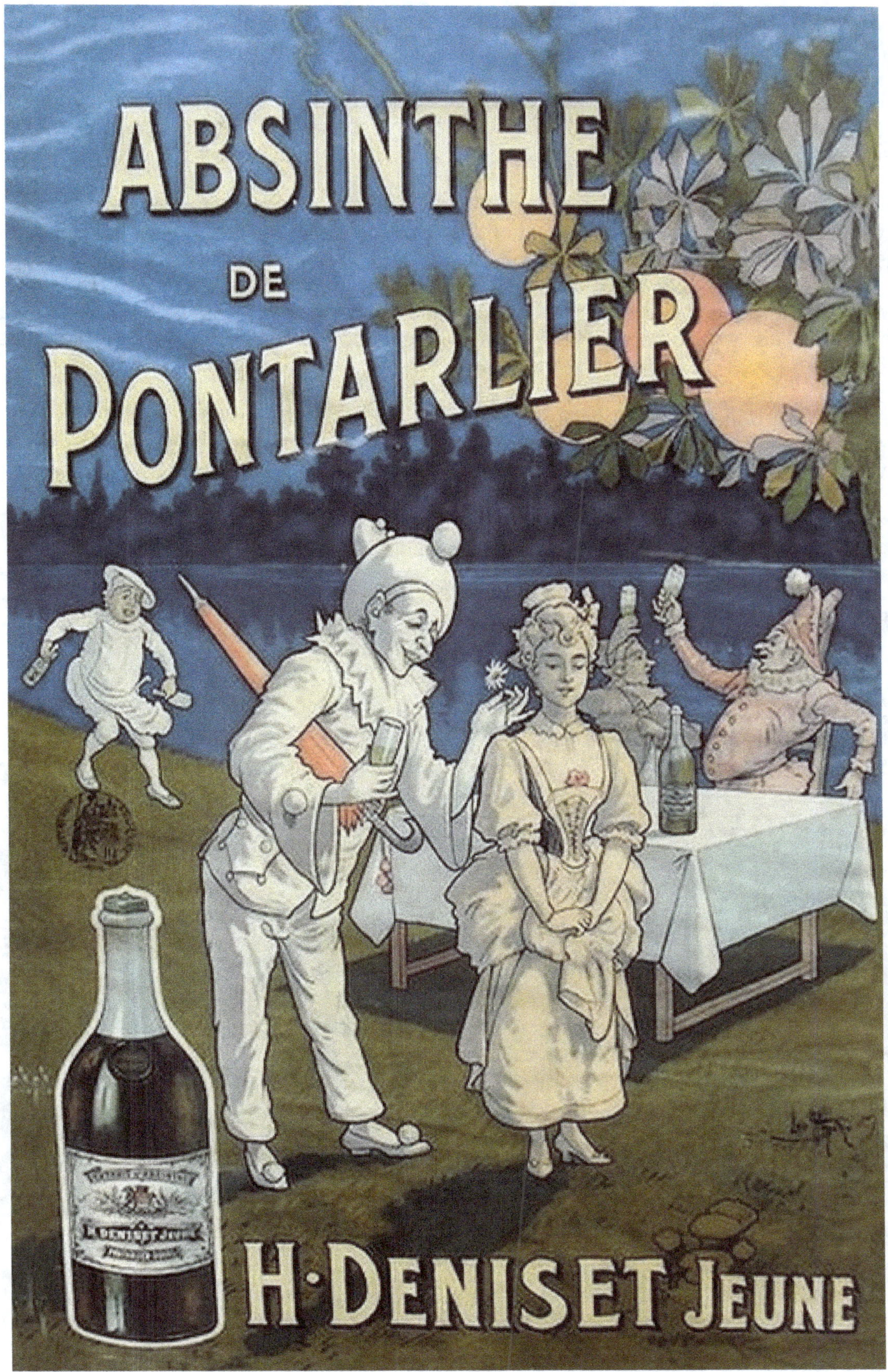

Marcellin Auzolle - Absinthe de Pontarlier, 1900

Edvard Munch (1863-1944) was a Norwegian painter whose 1893 work The Scream has become one of Western art's most acclaimed images.

He suffered from severe mental health difficulties during his lifetime and is believed to have had Borderline Personality Disorder. He displayed impulsive behaviour, which is a trait associated with alcoholism.

Like artists in Paris and other European cities, Munch lived a bohemian lifestyle. He was influenced by the Norwegian writer, philosopher, and anarchist political activist Hans Jaeger as part of a group known as the Kristiania Bohemians (Kristiania being the old name for the city of Oslo).

Munch was encouraged by Jaeger to express his emotions and his psychological state in his paintings, known as 'soul painting'. It was from this encouragement that his own unique style of emerged.

He arrived in Paris during the Exposition Universelle of 1889. He studied under Léon Bonnat in the mornings and spent his afternoons at exhibitions, galleries, and museums where he was impressed with the vast display of modern European art.

He was particularly impressed by the work of Paul Gaugin, Vincent Van Gogh, and Henri de Toulouse-Lautrec, especially their use of colour to convey emotion.

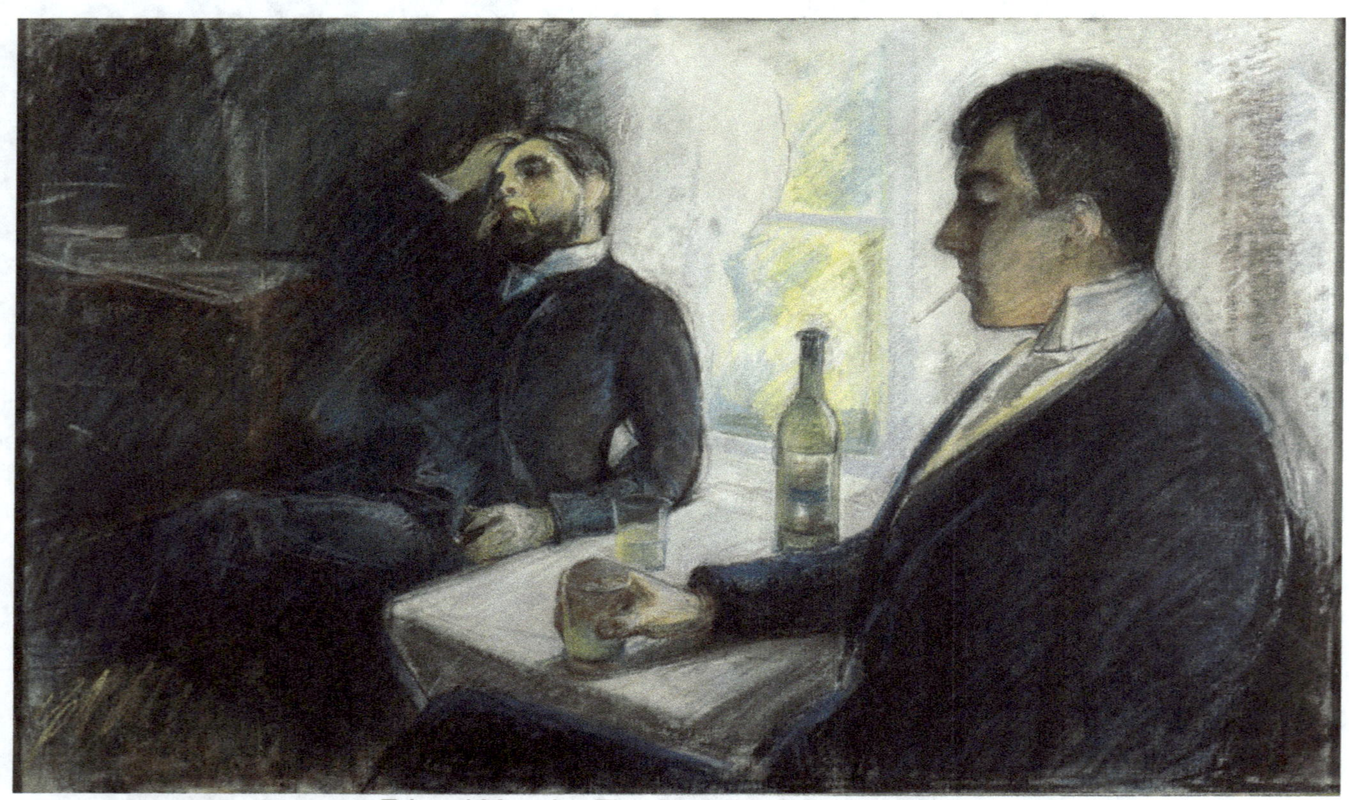

Edvard Munch - The Absinthe Drinkers, 1890

Viktor Oliva (1861-1928) was a Czech painter and illustrator born in Bohemia, Austria-Hungary. At the age of 17 he attended the Academy of Fine Arts, Prague and studied under František Sequens, who respected his work greatly. He continued his studies at the Munich Academy.

In 1888 he travelled to Montmartre, Paris to be a part of the expanding artistic community. This was hugely inspirational for Oliva and his art greatly improved in such a rich artistic environment.

He became good friends with other Bohemian Parisians such as Luděk Marold, Mikoláš Aleš, Jakub Arbes, and Karel Vítězslav Mašek.

In 1897 he became the Images Editor of the popular Czech language magazine *Zlatá Praha* (Golden Prague), a post which he held for 19 years.

He was also commissioned to create many dramatic works including the ceilings of several buildings in Bohemia, and he also had several works hanging in his favourite cafe, Café Slavia, which still displays his most famous work *Piják Absintu* (The Absinthe Drinker).

Pablo Picasso (1881-1973) was a Spanish painter, sculptor, printmaker, ceramicist, and theatre designer who spent most of his life in France.

He was inspired by Henri Matisse to explore more radical styles, which resulted in a fruitful rivalry between the two, who were often collectively described by art critics as two leaders of modern art.

Picasso arrived in Paris in 1901, and his works from that point until 1904 are described as his blue period. He painted several subjects drinking absinthe, characterised by shades of blue and green, only occasionally warmed by other colours.

Often described as sombre or melancholy, they are among his most popular works in modern times, which he had difficulty selling at the time.

He was greatly affected by his travel through Spain, and by the suicide of his friend Carles Casagemas, who took his own life at L'Hippodrome Café in Paris.

Suffering from depression, Picasso chose to express a sense of melancholy, loneliness, and despair felt by the impoverished outsiders of society, which was not the kind of subject that art buyers were interested in at the time, and his financial situation deteriorated.

Like Édouard Manet's Absinthe Drinker of 1859, and Edgar Degas's Absinthe Drinker of 1876, Picasso's absinthe drinkers reflected a reality of some peoples' lives that art critics and art buyers were not willing to entertain.

The fact that absinthe played a role in these paintings inadvertently reinforced the stereotype among those who disapproved of them, that absinthe was a symbol of decadence and moral decay.

The artists who did enjoy absinthe as part of their social circle embraced its notoriety. They were inspired by the experience of drinking absinthe at social events with its stimulative and sedative effects, combined with the stimulating discussions about the arts that flowed along with them.

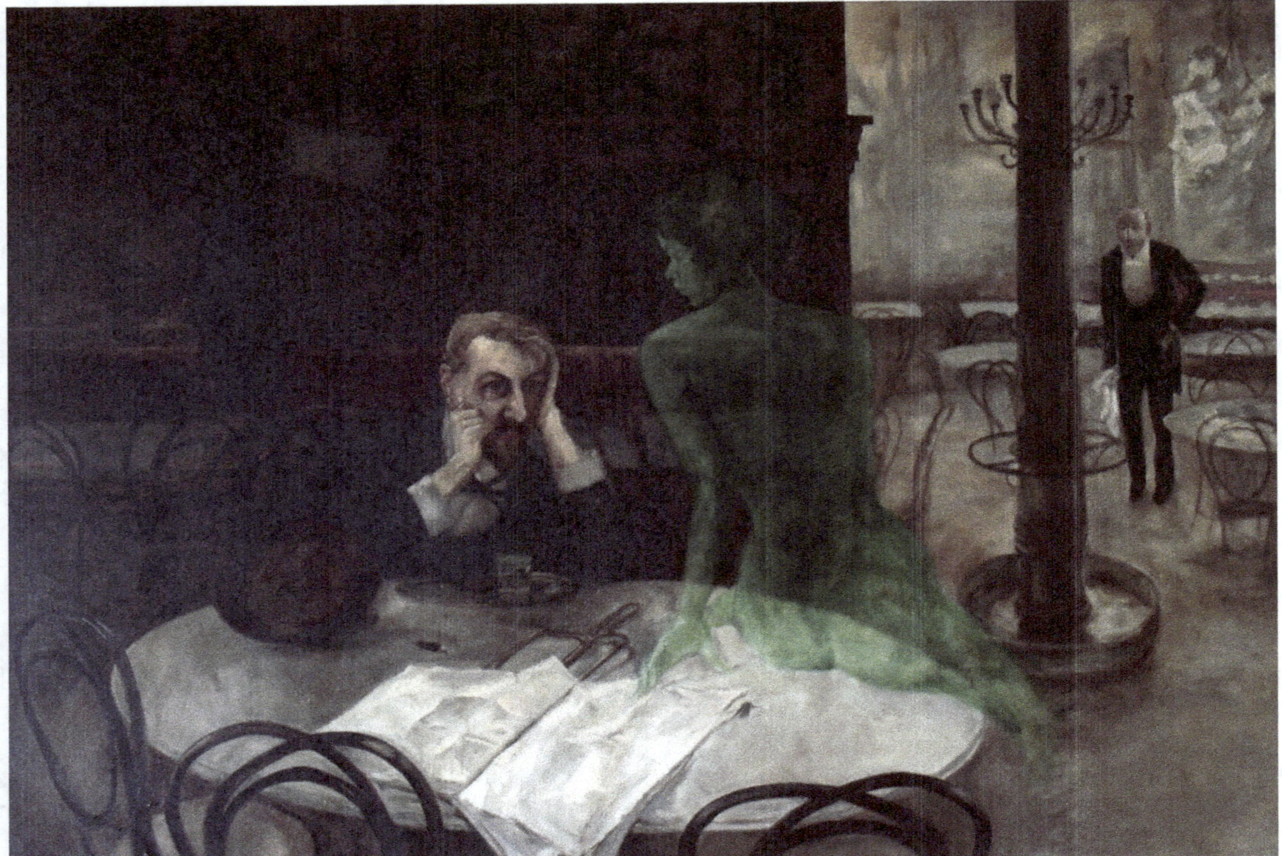

Viktor Oliva - The Absinthe Drinker, 1901

The Absinthe Drinker is depicted in a café, late at night, being visited by the Green Fairy (also known by artists as the Green Muse and by Aleister Crowley as the Green Goddess). The drinker is clearly enthralled by her presence. All of the other customers have long since gone, and the only other person who remains is the waiter in the background. The waiter is either on his way over to remind the drinker that it is closing time, or perhaps he is surprised to be able to see the Green Fairy too, and he is watching from a distance, stunned, as she sits on the table looking over the drinker.

She represents artistic enlightenment and exploration, poetic inspiration, a freer state of mind, new ideas, or perhaps a symbol of a change of social order. A symbol of transformation, she is a trusted guide on the journey to artistic innovation, to lead the drinker away from the conventional reality of the here and now, to escape into the sanctuary of the surreal. Some say that having been summoned by the absinthe ritual; she first appears dancing in the glass. As the ice cold drops of water fall into the reservoir, the transformation of the green liquid into a milky misty light green haze is her arrival.

Perhaps one of the most famous quotes regarding the experience of absinthe is that of Oscar Wilde:

> *"After the first glass you see things as you wish they were.*
> *After the second, you see things as they are not.*
> *Finally you see things as they really are,*
> *and that is the most horrible thing in the world"*

This quote does not appear in any of Wilde's works or letters, but was recounted by Ada Laverson in Letters to the Sphinx From Oscar Wilde, with Reminiscences of the Author in 1930, and John Fothergill in his book My Three Inns in 1949.

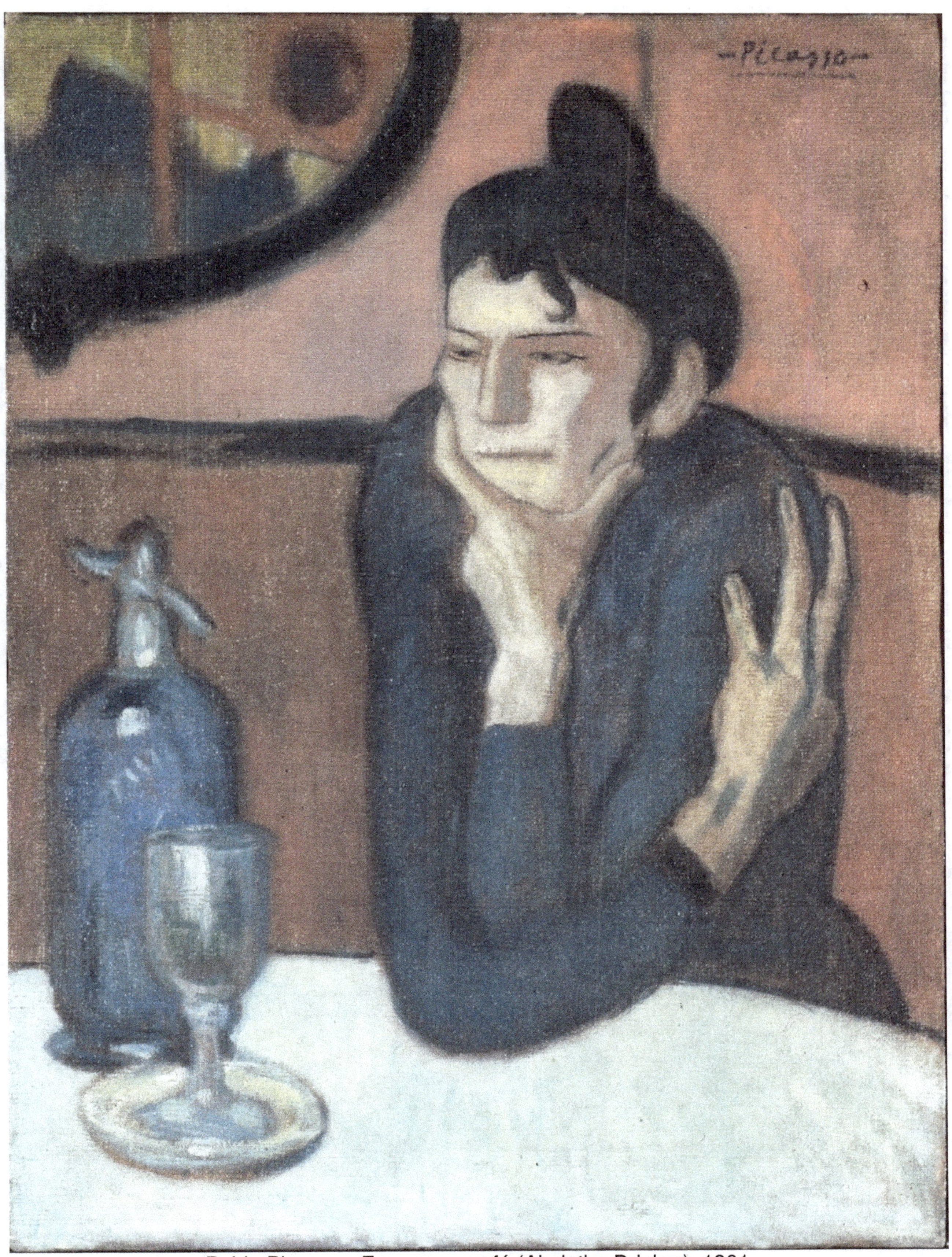

Pablo Picasso - Femme au café (Absinthe Drinker), 1901

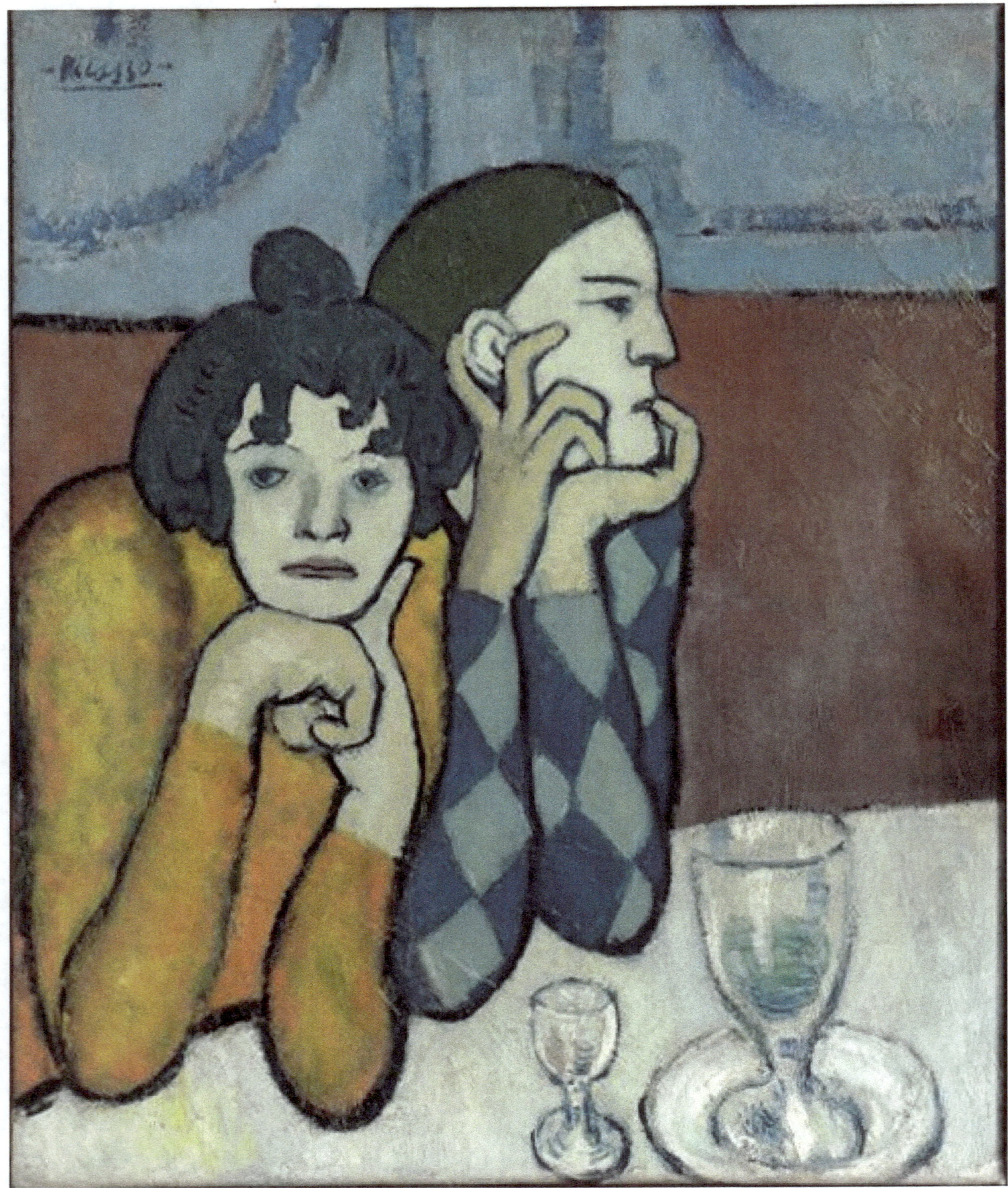

Picasso - Harlequin and his Companion, 1901

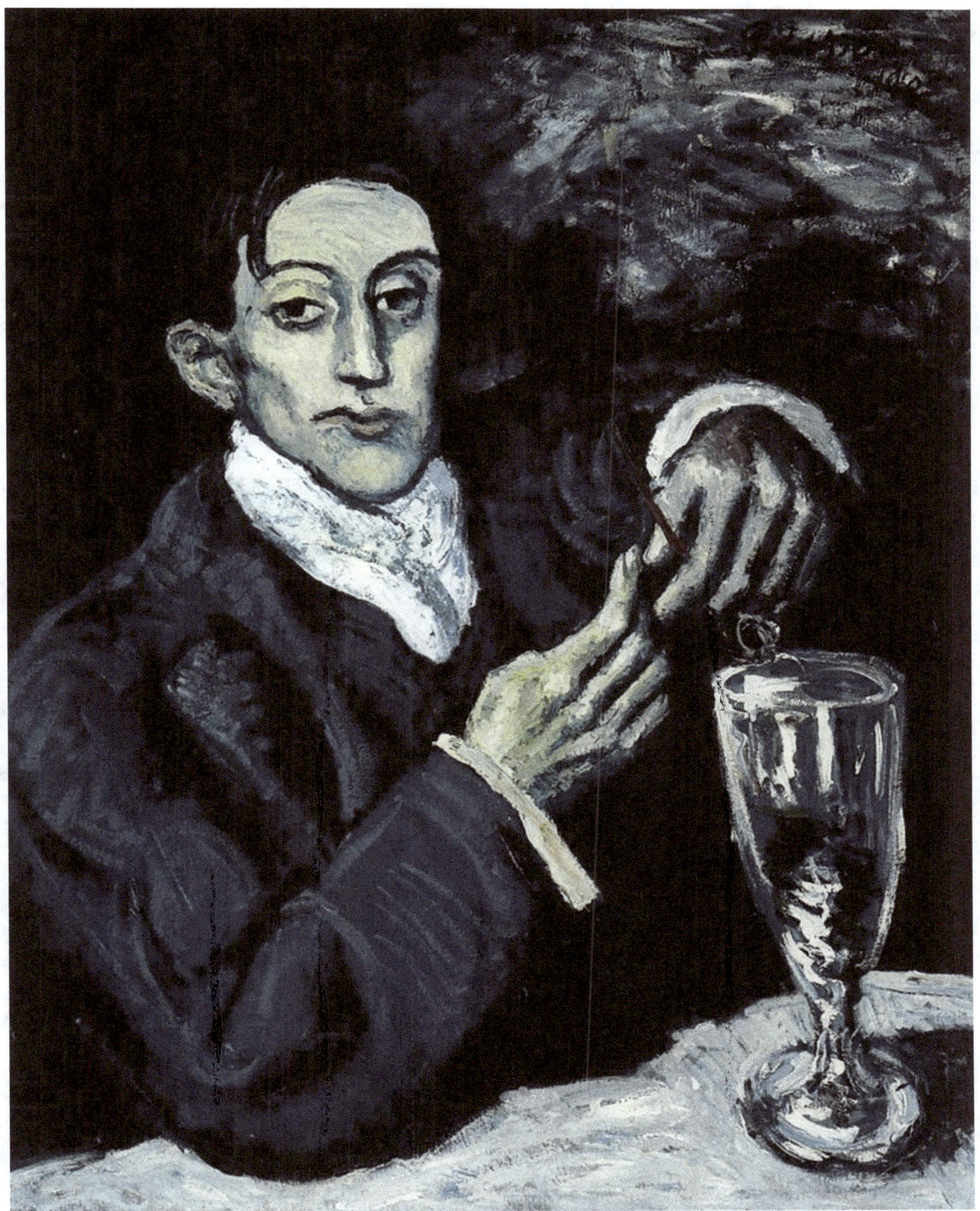

Pablo Picasso - Angel Fernández de Soto with absinthe, 1903

"Anti-alcoholics are unfortunates in the grip of water, that terrible poison, so corrosive that out of all substances it has been chosen for washing and scouring, and a drop of water added to a clear liquid like Absinthe, muddles it".

Alfred Jarry (1873-1907)
symbolist writer

Jean Béraud (1849-1934) was a painter who was well known for his paintings depicting the life of Paris society. His works are described as somewhere between the academic style of the Salon and the Impressionists, gradually shifting towards Impressionism.

His paintings often included a sense of mockery of Parisian life at the time. His work was largely ignored until after the Russian Revolution when Russian artists embraced his work with irony, interpreting them as the embodiment of Western commercialism and the bourgeois tastes of the rich middle classes.

In several of Béraud's paintings depicting people in brasseries, bistros, and cafés, absinthe can be seen Many of the subjects depicted drinking absinthe have a wistful daydreaming look on their faces, often looking away from their companions as if staring into the distance.

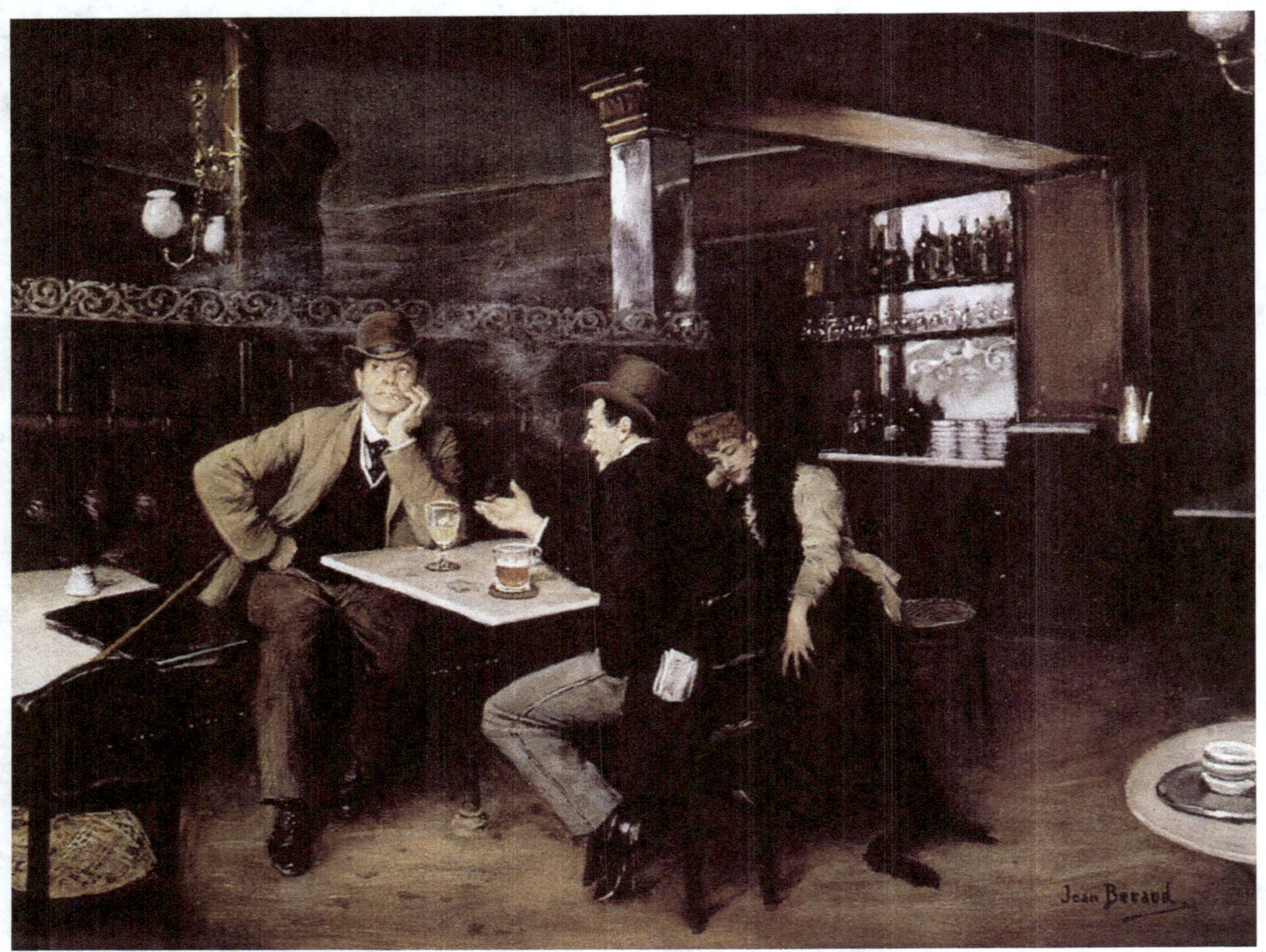

1891 Jean Beraud - L'Ennui Boredom, 1891

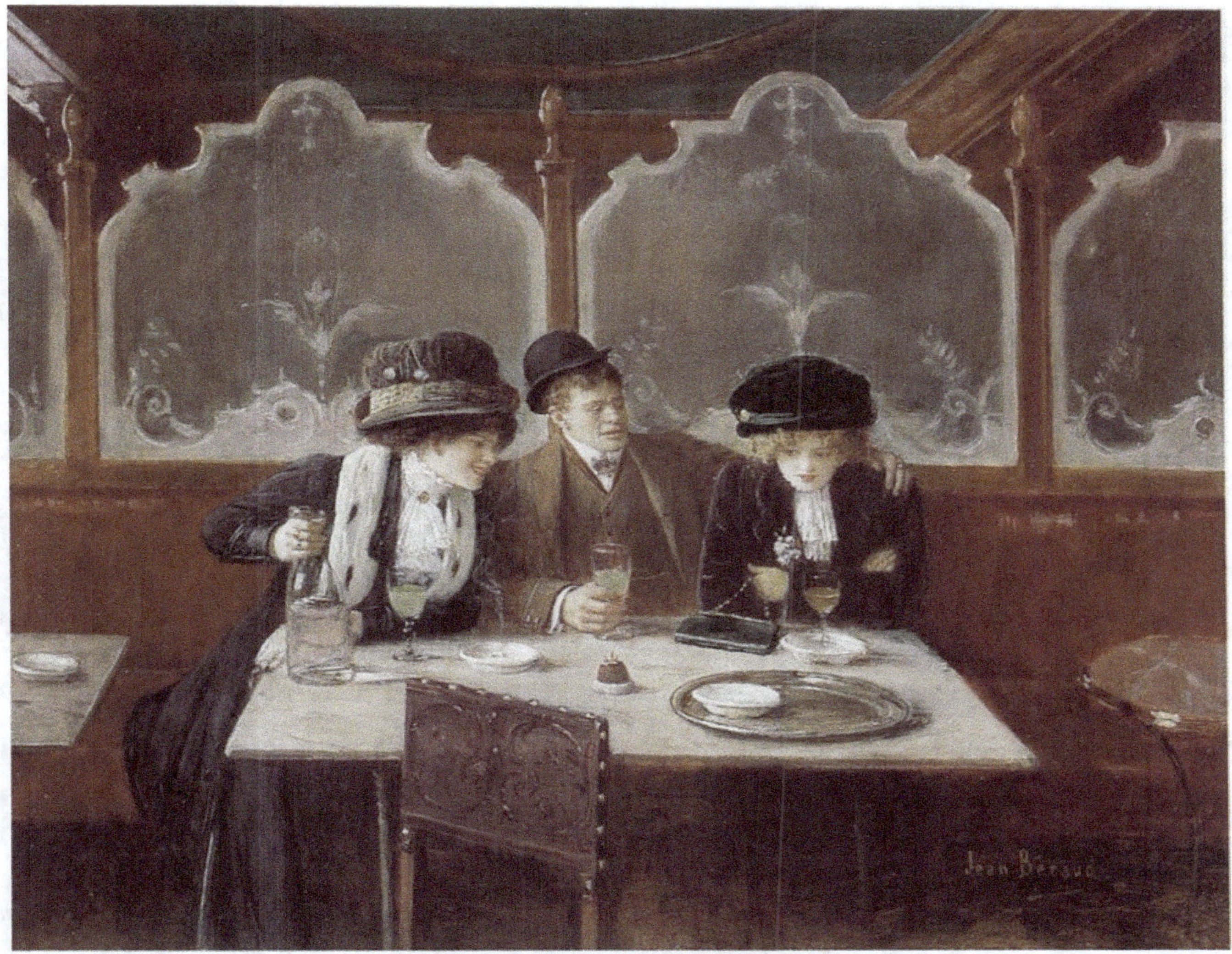

1908 Jean Beraud - Au Cafe, c1908

"I am the green Fairy
My robe is the colour of despair
I have nothing in common with the fairies of the past
What I need is blood, red and hot,
The palpitating flesh of my victims
Alone, I will kill France, the present is dead,
Vive the future...
But me, I kill the future and in family I destroy
The love of country, courage, honour,
I am the purveyor of hell, penitentiaries, hospitals.
Who am I finally?
I am the instigator of crime
I am ruin and sorrow
I am shame
I am dishonour
I am death
I am Absinthe"

In am the Green Fairy, Marie Corelli, 1890

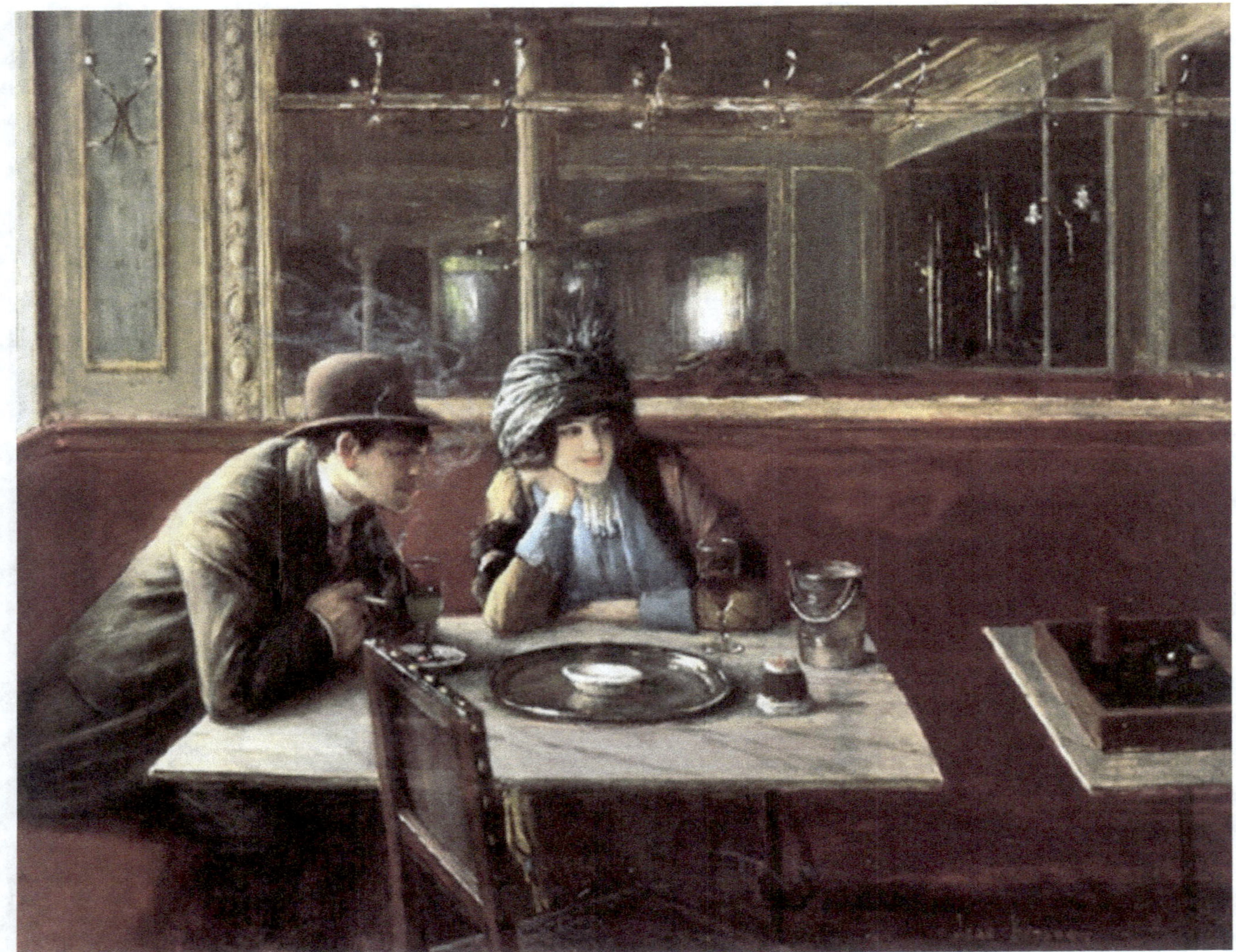

1908 Jean Beraud - Au Cafe, c1908

"Absinthe, mother of all happiness, O
infinite liquor, you glint in my glass
green and pale like the eyes of the
mistress I once loved. Absinthe, mother
of happiness, like Her, you leave in the
body a memory of distant pain; absinthe,
mother of insane rages and of staggering
drunkenness, where one can say without
thinking oneself mad that one is loved
by one's mistress. Absinthe, your
fragrance smoothes me..."

Absinthe, Gustave Kahn

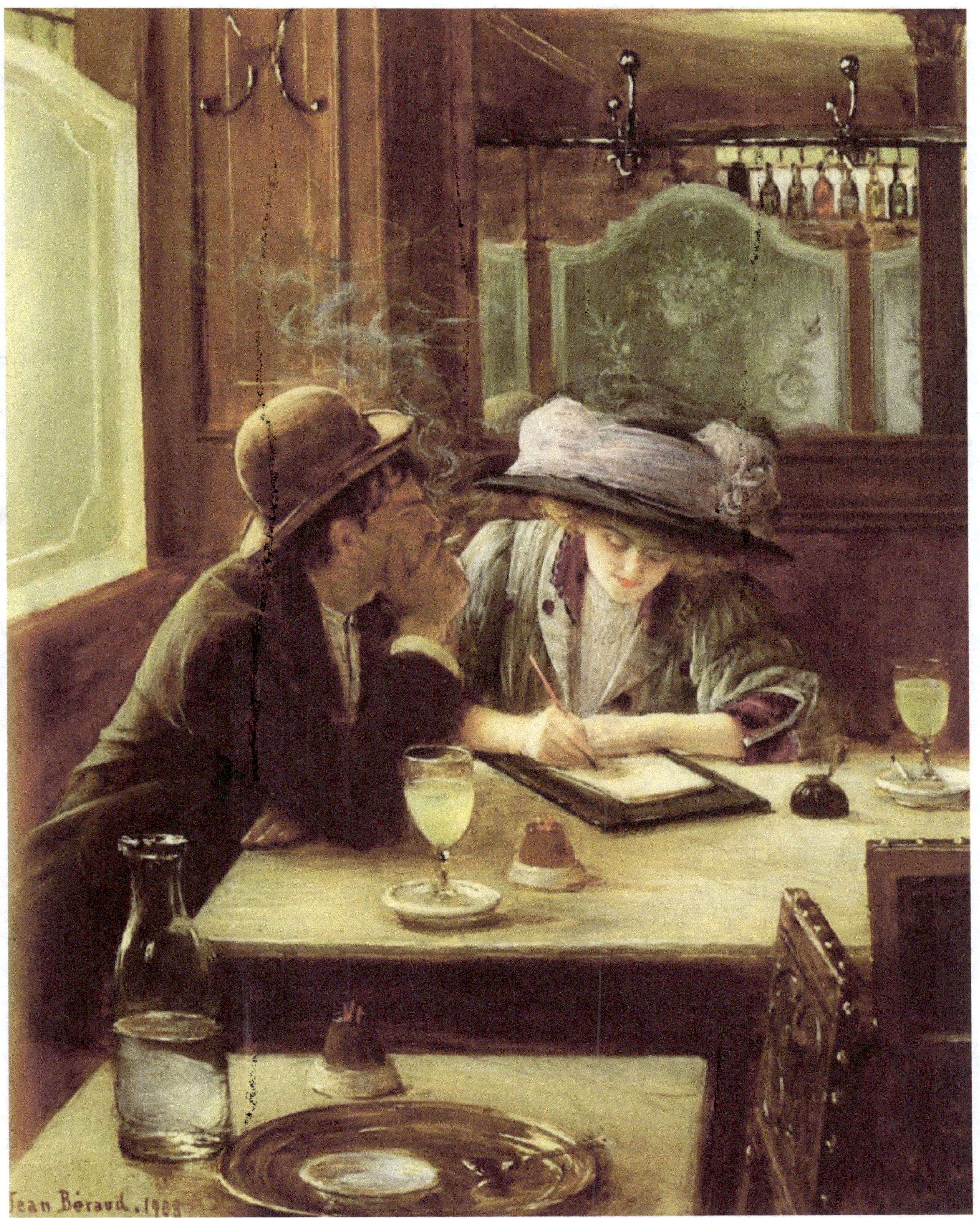

1908 Jean Beraud - La Lettre, 1908

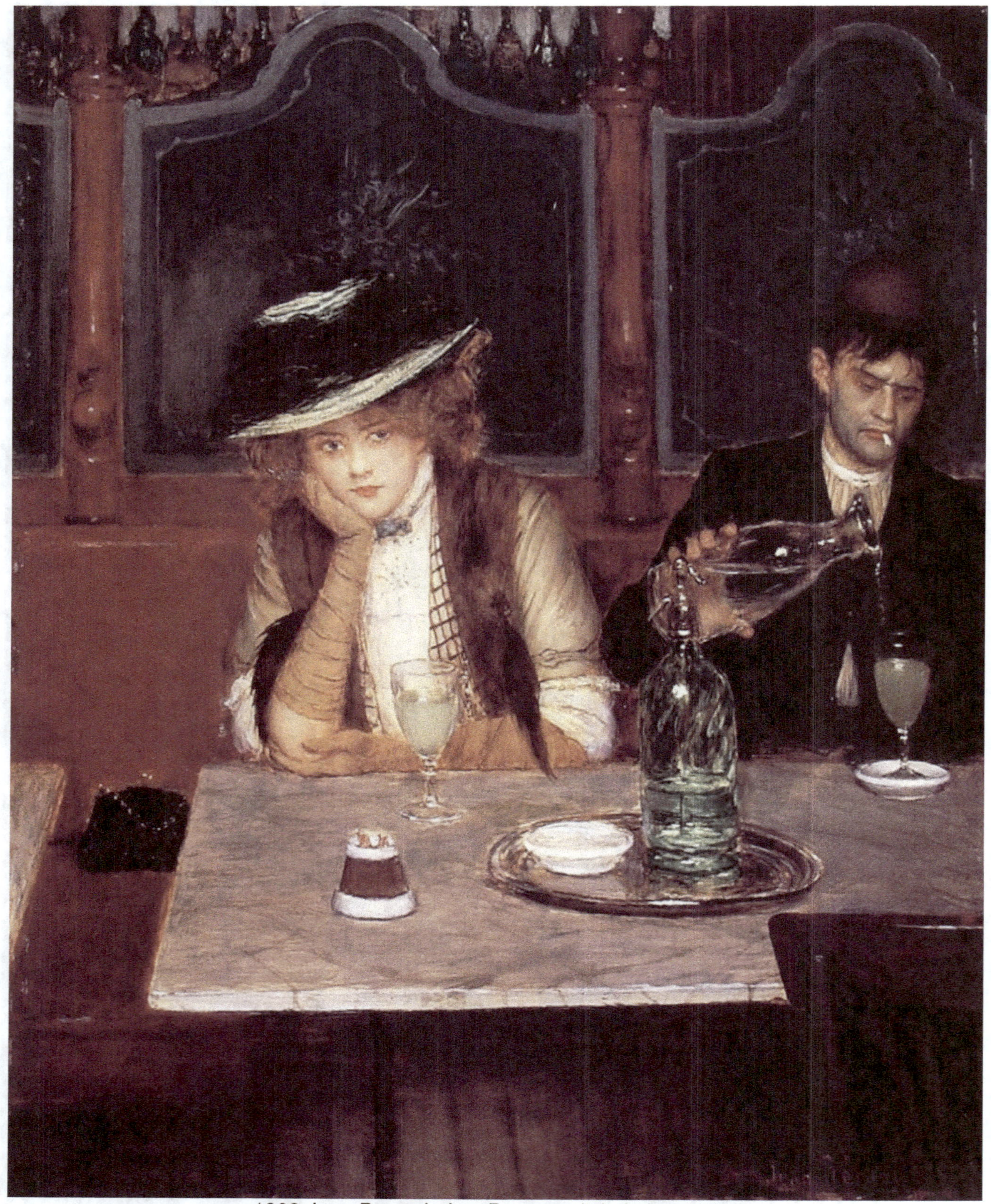

1908 Jean Beraud - Les Buveurs d'absinthe, 1908

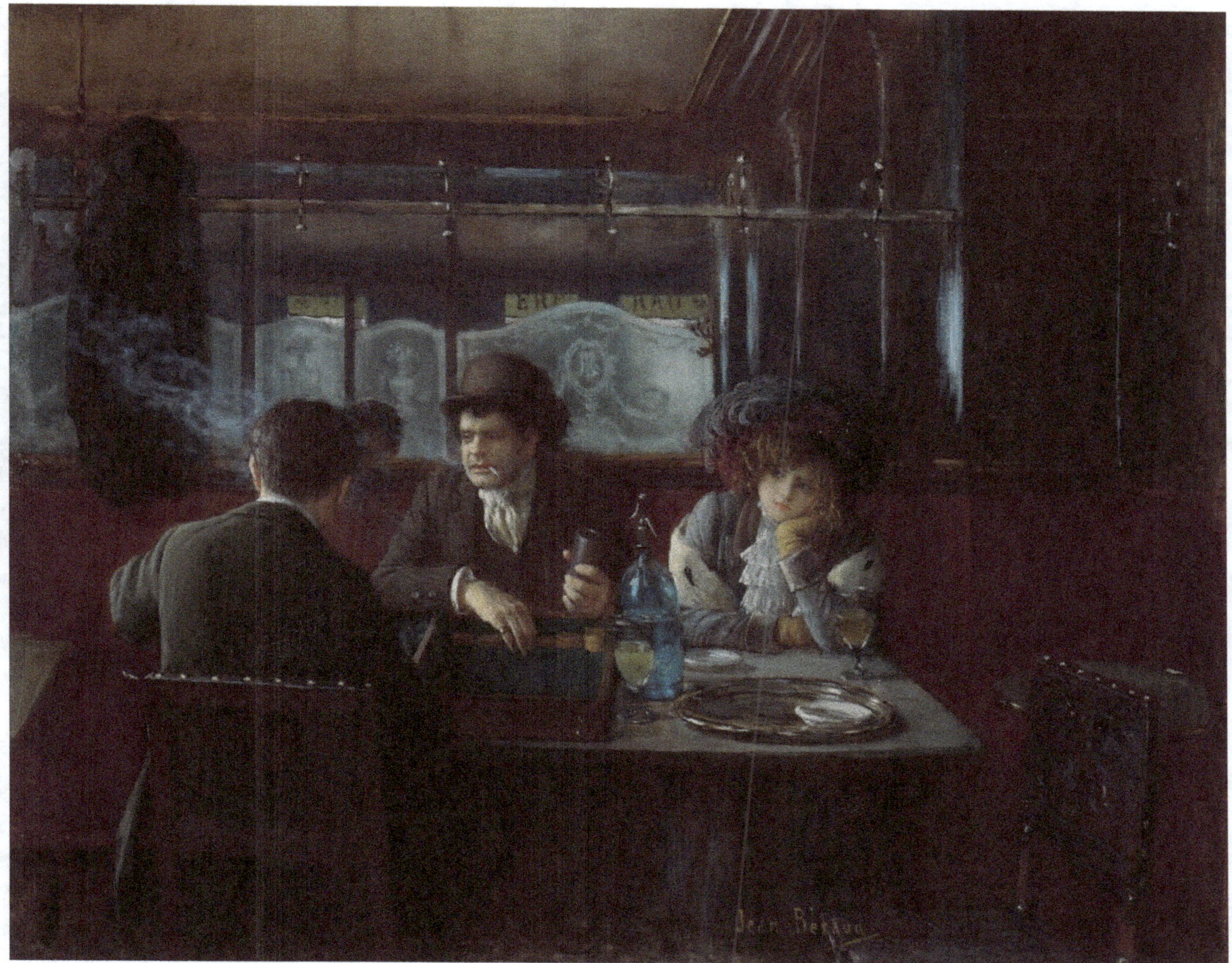

1909 Jean Beraud - Au Cafe, La Partie de jacquet Backgammon, 1909

"Absinthe, I adore you truly!
It seems when I drink you,
I inhale the young forest's soul,
During the beautiful green season.

Your perfume disconcerts me
And in your opalescence
I see the full heavens of yore,
As through an open door.

What matter, O refuge of the damned!
That you a vain paradise be,
If you appease my need;

And if, before I enter the door,
You make me put up with life,
By accustoming me to death."

L'Absinthe, Raoul Ponchon

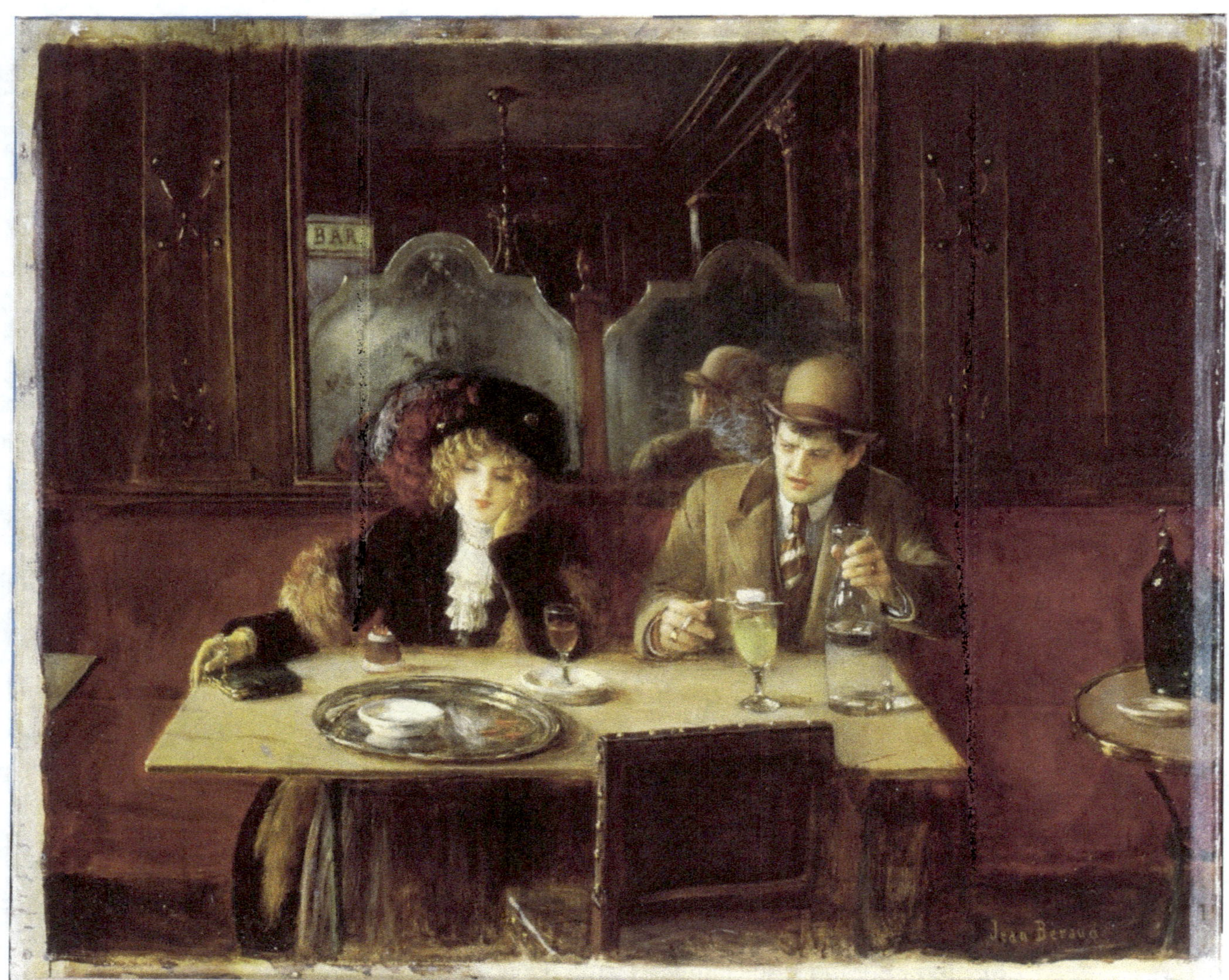
1909 Jean Beraud - Le Couple au Cafe, 1909

"Gently I wave the visible world away.
Far off, I hear a roar, afar yet near,
Far off and strange, a voice is in my ear,
And is the voice my own? the words I say
Fall strangely, like a dream, across the day;
And the dim sunshine is a dream. How clear,
New as the world to lovers' eyes, appear
The men and women passing on their way!

The world is very fair. The hours are all
Linked in a dance of mere forgetfulness.
I am at peace with God and man. O glide,
Sands of the hour-glass that I count not, fall
Serenely: scarce I feel your soft caress.
Rocked on this dreamy and indifferent tide."

The Absinthe Drinker, Arthur Sýmons, 1892

6.   The Green Curse and the Ban

Alcoholism

What made absinthe unique was that it allowed (or trusted) the consumer to decide by how much it was diluted for taste and strength, if at all. It was therefore easier to misuse to excess, and perhaps it was even sought out for misuse because of its strength before dilution.

The misuse of alcohol is as old as alcohol itself, and as alcoholism became increasingly defined as a social issue, absinthe being the strongest alcohol available came to symbolise alcoholism as a whole, and by 1911, France was the largest consumer of alcohol in the world.

Vincent Van Gogh

Vincent Van Gogh is one of the most famous and influential figures in the history of Western art. He suffered with mental illness and depression for much of his life, including psychotic episodes and delusions, and spending time in psychiatric hospitals. He cut off part of his ear with a razor in a rage during a confrontation with his former friend and colleague Paul Gaugin.

Some have suggested he had bipolar disorder, some have suggested acute intermittent porphyria, some have suggested temporal lobe epilepsy, whatever the nature of his illness, it was likely worsened by malnutrition, overwork, insomnia, and alcohol.

He drank many different types of alcohol, of which absinthe was just one part. The assumption that it was absinthe alone was part of the notoriety that brought about the banning of absinthe.

The Great Wine Blight

The vineyards of France suffered a severe blight in the 1860s which struck a devastating blow to the wine industry. Attempts to grow French grape vines in the American colonies had proved unsuccessful.

American grape vines had a resistance to their local pests that French grape vines did not, and research was conducted to try and find something of the American vine that could be transplanted or grafted into French vines to give them the required resistance to grow successfully in America.

The transportation of goods across the Atlantic Ocean was accelerating thanks to the improving technology of steam ships. Unfortunately this quicker transportation allowed a greater chance for the survival of pests, such as aphids like Phylloxera, which were inadvertently introduced to Europe.

French botanist Jules Émile Planchon discovered Phylloxera as the source of the blight, and grafting techniques were used to fortify or reconstitute European vines in order to protect them.

Meanwhile absinthe manufacturers switched from using grape based alcohol to beet or grain based alcohol, which made it cheaper still.

The wine industry and the temperance movement now had a common enemy in absinthe, and some even claimed that exaggerated and fabricated claims and smear campaigns did much to spur a trend in the association of absinthe with violent crimes and social disorder[10].

---

[10] *Wittels, Betina J.; Breaux, T.A. (2017). Absinthe: The Exquisite Elixir. Fulcrum Publishing. p. 45. ISBN 978-1682750018.*

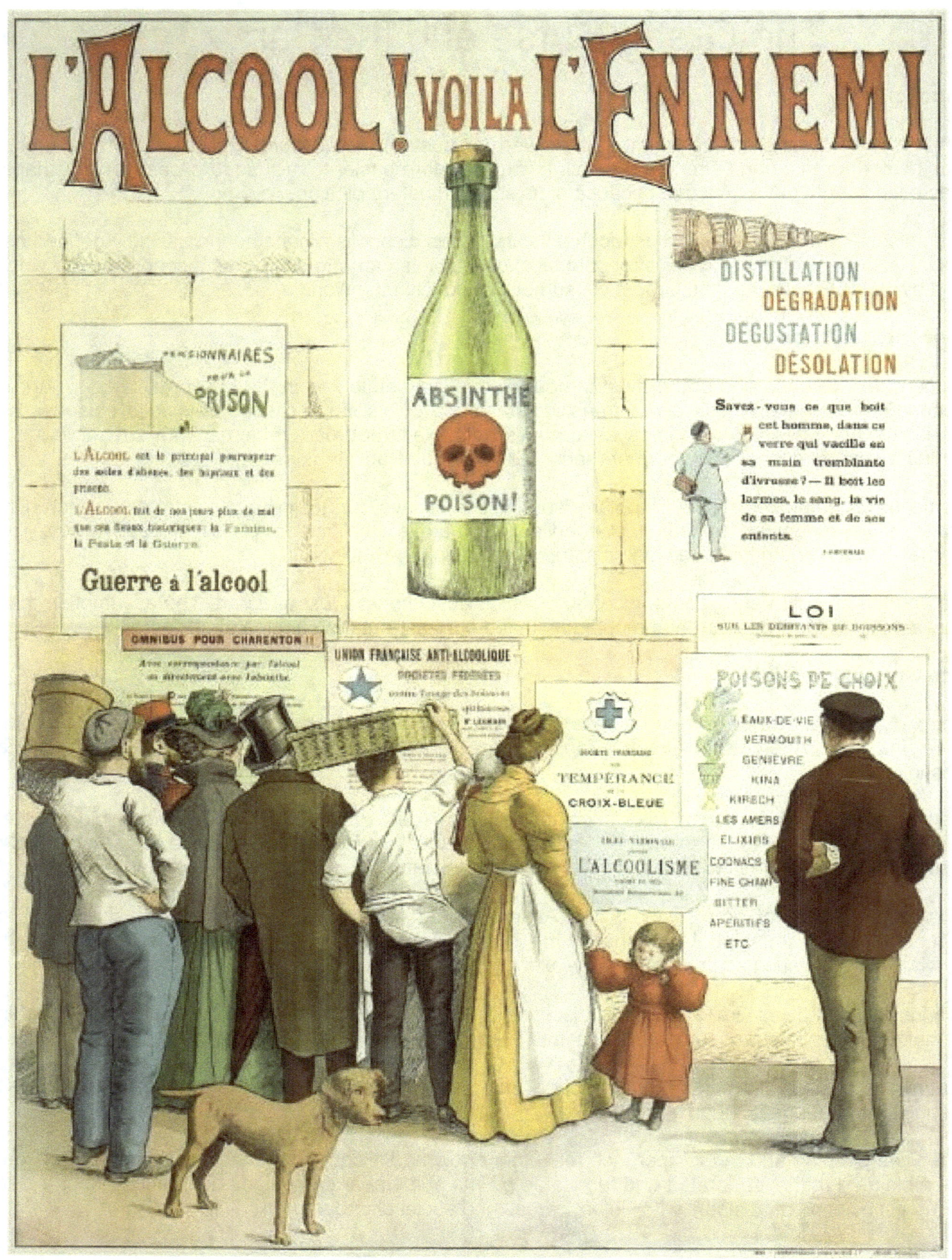

Frederic Christol - L'Alcool, Voila L'Ennemi, 1910

The Temperance Movement

By the early 1900s the Temperance Movement had gained ground and grown into a mass social movement supported by doctors and politicians. Voluntary moderation, self restraint, and abstinence were promoted as the way to protect the moral fabric of society.

Participants warned of alcohol's negative effects on health and family life, claiming that it was responsible for tuberculosis, mental illness, domestic abuse, and crime. It would only be a matter of time before a tragic case would be seized upon as representative of the problem as a whole. Absinthe was the strongest, and therefore the worst demon of them all.

In popular culture, the burgeoning motion picture film industry provided a cautionary tale about the dangers of absinthe in the 1914 American silent film written and directed by Herbert Brenon. Simply titled 'Absinthe', it tells the story of Parisian artist Jean Dumas (played by King Baggot) who becomes addicted to absinthe and sinks into a life of robbery and murder.

The Case of Jean Lanfray

On the 28th August 1905 in Commugny, Switzerland, Jean Lanfray, a Swiss-French farm labourer, drank a total of seven glasses of wine, six glasses of cognac, two coffees laced with brandy, two crème de menthes, and two glasses of absinthe. Later at home he flew into a drunken rage and murdered his pregnant wife and two children.

In the trial that followed several months later, Lanfray's lawyers argued that the two ounces of absinthe consumed prior to the murders were solely to blame for his actions[11]. Swiss psychologist Dr Albert Maiham testified that Lanfray suffered "a classic case of absinthe madness".

The prosecutor Alfred Obrist argued that the two ounces of absinthe he had ingested were minor in relation to the large amounts of other alcoholic beverages that he had consumed that day, but as far as many people were concerned… it was the *absinthe* that made him do it.

The Science

It was believed that the thujone in absinthe caused effects that were discernibly different from those of alcoholism alone, and thus the term absinthism[12] was coined, referring to a dazed confused state with terrifying hallucinations. Now all that was needed was some science to prove it.

Thujone had long been known to cause convulsions and seizures in high doses. All one had to do was overestimate or exaggerate the amount of thujone in absinthe to make the case that it contained dangerously high levels.

In 1864 French psychiatrist Valentin Magnan conducted an experiment with two guinea pigs. One was exposed to large doses of pure wormwood vapour, the other to alcohol vapours. The guinea pig exposed to wormwood vapours experienced convulsive seizures, while the one exposed to alcohol vapours did not. Magnan blamed thujone for these effects[13].

Absinthe was thought to contain up to 260-350 milligrams per litre, and as such it was portrayed as a dangerously addictive psychoactive drug and hallucinogen. Modern tests have shown that previous estimates were in fact far too high.

---

[11] *Conrad III, Barnaby; (1988). Absinthe History in a Bottle. Chronicle books. ISBN 0811816508 pp. 1–4*
[12] *Padosch SA, Lachenmeier DW, Kröner LU. Absinthism: a fictitious 19th century syndrome with present impact. Subst Abuse Treat Prev Policy. 2006 May 10;1:14. doi: 10.1186/1747-597X-1-14. PMID: 16722551; PMCID: PMC1475830.*
[13] *Conrad III, Barnaby; (1988). Absinthe: History in a Bottle. Chronicle Books. ISBN 0811816508 p. 101*

A 2008 study of 13 bottles from 1895-1910 using gas chromatography-mass spectrometry (GC-MS) found that the bottles had between 0.5 and 48.3 milligrams of thujone per litre, averaging at around 25.4 milligrams of thujone per litre.

A 2005 study recreated three high-wormwood recipes from 1899 and tested with GC-MS, and found that the highest contained 4.3 milligrams per litre of thujone.

There is no direct evidence that thujone causes hallucinations, and absinthe has not been demonstrated to be any more dangerous than ordinary spirits, and any psychoactive properties (apart from those of alcohol) have been wildly exaggerated.

Lack of Regulation and Inferior Imitations

Other spirits such as whisky, brandy, and gin are globally defined and regulated. Even today only Switzerland has a legal definition of what absinthe is and how it must be produced by the distillation process in order to be called absinthe. This meant that producers were free to label a product as 'absinthe' or 'absinth' without regard to any specific legal definition or quality standards.

Absinthe was big business, and in order to cash in, cheaper imitations by unscrupulous producers flooded the marketplace. Shortcuts were taken which produced dangerous results. Copper salts, which are toxic, were added to the mixture to artificially enhance the green glow.

Home production in copper baths contaminated the process, especially when cheaper inferior alcohol was used which was contaminated with methanol. Antimony trichloride was also used to fake the cloudy louche effect when combined with water.

The Petition and the Ban

After the case of Jean Lanfray, a petition to ban absinthe in Switzerland gained 82,000 signatures. A referendum was held on the 5th July 1908[14], and the ban took effect on the 7th October 1910. Similar incidents led to absinthe being banned in the rest of Europe and in the United States:

Congo Free State	1898	The United States	1912
Belgium	1906	France	1914
Brazil	1906	Finland	1919
The Netherlands	1909	Germany	1923
Switzerland	1910	Italy	1932

Absinthe was not banned in Britain because it had not reached anywhere near the same level of mass popularity as it had on the continent. It was also not banned in the Czech Republic, Norway and Sweden, or Spain and Portugal.

After the ban and the end of the First World War, Pernod Fils moved their production from France to Catalonia where absinthe was still legal. Sales gradually declined into obscurity until production was stopped in the 1960s.

In Switzerland absinthe production was driven underground and produced without the green colouring. With its clear colourless appearance it became known as 'blanche' (white) or 'bleu' (blue). In this form it was also easier to disguise as other spirits to avoid detection by the authorities.

---

[14] Nohlen, D & Stöver, P. (2010) *Elections in Europe: A Data Dandbook*, p. 1906 ISBN 978-3832956097

The Bohemian Style 'Absinth'

In the Czech Republic, Spain, and Portugal, the Bohemian style of 'absinth' emerged which favours cold mixing rather than traditional distillation.

Consisting of a blend of flavours and colourings in alcohol, there was less emphasis on the anise flavour, and no cloudy louche effect when the water was added.

A new ritual emerged to add theatricality to this Bohemian style of absinth. The sugar cube soaked and placed on the spoon was set alight instead of being dripped upon and broken down gradually.

It was then put out with water and stirred into the glass, with the caramelised dissolving sugar resembling a kind of substitute cloudy louche effect.

The flaming technique burned off some of the alcohol, which meant that the ratio of absinthe to water was reduced to 1:1 in order to maintain the same balance of strength and flavour as traditional absinthe.

The Arrival of Pastis

Pastis emerged some 17 years after the ban on absinthe, at a time when France was still apprehensive of high alcohol drinks after the moral panic of the absinthe ban. It was first commercialised by Paul Ricard in 1932 and is still massively popular in France to this day.

Unlike absinthe, pastis does not contain wormwood, and the main anise flavour comes from star anise and liquorice root instead of green anise and fennel. Some brands of pastis such as Henri Bardouin have a fascinatingly complex flavour with over 65 different herbs and spices, a third of which are kept secret.

Part of the popularity of pastis may be due to satisfying a penchant for anise flavoured spirits cultivated over generations by absinthe. It also connects with a wider and older tradition of anise flavoured spirits and liqueurs all across the Mediterranean, such as sambuca, ouzo, arak, raki, anisette, and mastika.

They are traditionally distilled between 40%-50% by volume (80-100 proof) and enjoyed as a long and refreshing drink with ice water, served at a ratio of 5 parts water to 1 part pastis.

The name pastis comes from the Occitan word *pastís* meaning a mash-up or blend. It is particularly popular in the Occitanian south-eastern region of France such as Marseille where it is strongly culturally associated with the variety of boules known as pétanque.

Such outdoor ball games have a strong social tradition in the region, and players of the game are often described in a humorous cliché as holding a pétanque ball in one hand and a glass of pastis in the other.

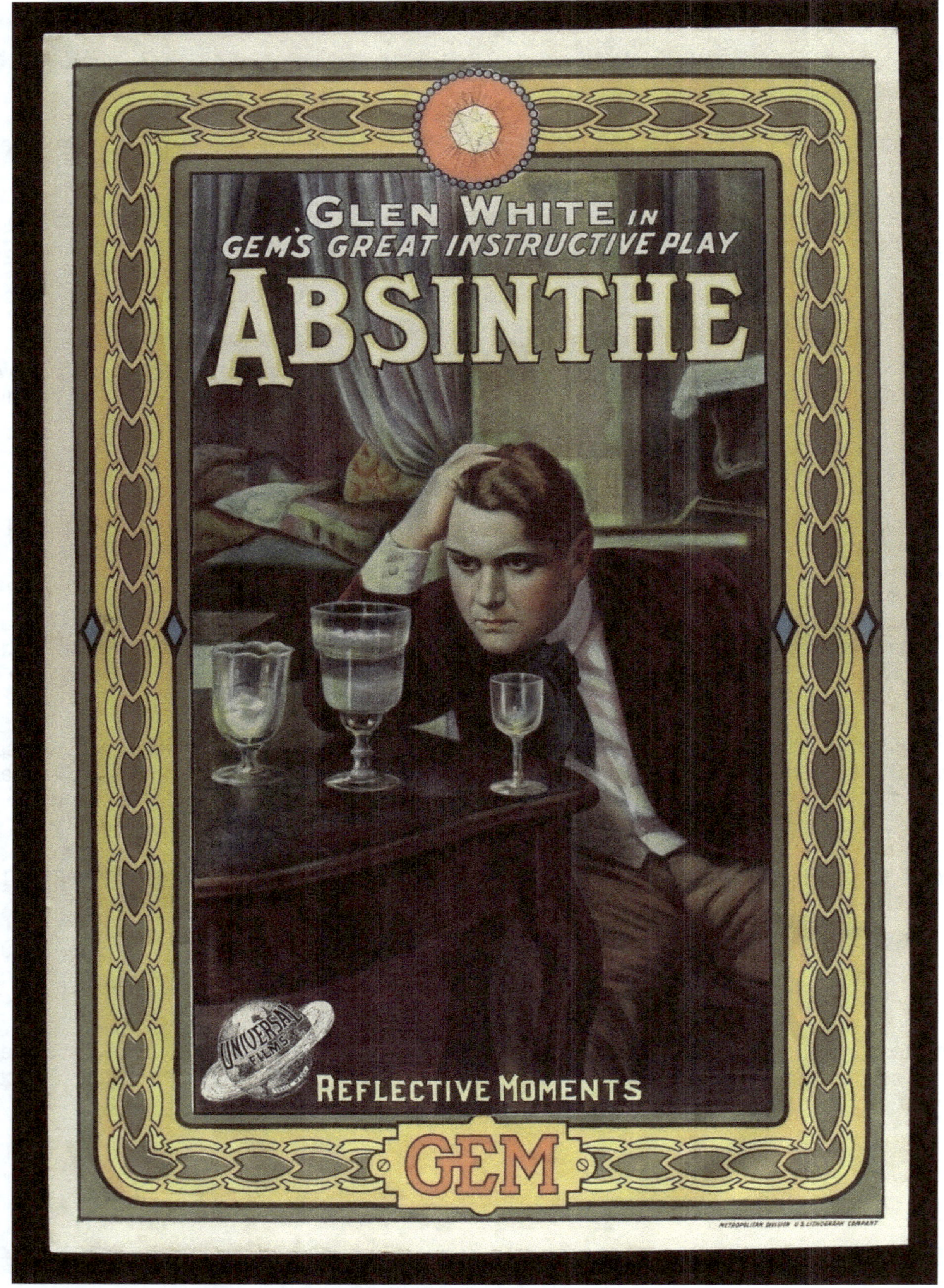

A poster for the film Absinthe, 1914

7.　　The Revival

On the 22nd June 1988, the European Union issued Council Directive 88/388/EEC relating to flavourings for use in foodstuffs and source materials for their production. Right at the end of the document is "Thuyone" (Thujone) with the restriction "10 mg/kg in alcoholic beverages with more than 25% volume of alcohol".

In the 1990s, the British entrepreneur George Rowley spent some time in the Czech Republic where he experienced Bohemian style absinth, which had not been banned. In 1996 he founded Bohemia Beer House Ltd (later BBH Spirits) and imported several alcoholic drinks to the UK.

In 1998 BBH Spirits applied the EU directive 88/388/EEC to the production of absinthe, where it was approved by UK Trading Standards in June 1998. BBH Spirits then began importing Hill's Absinth made by Czech company Hill's Liquere into the UK.

The publicity and events that followed, including my own experience at the Golden Café in Soho's Golden Square, caused a renewed interest in this Bohemian style absinth with its eye catching flaming ritual, and opened the way for absinthe bans across Europe to be lifted, and for licensing, importing, and exporting to resume after nearly 100 years.

Absinthe purists and connoisseurs may have regarded these early revival products as inferior in quality and not representative of the original 19th century spirit, but this 'foot-in-the-door' paved the way for other brands to be produced and sold to a widening and increasingly informed new market.

In 2000, La Fée Absinthe became the first commercial absinthe distilled and bottled in France since the 1914 ban[15]. The ban was lifted in the Netherlands in 2004, and Belgium and Switzerland in 2005.

In 2007 the French brand Lucid became the first genuine absinthe to receive a Certificate of Label Approval for import into the United States since 1912, followed by the availability of the first American made absinthe St George Absinthe Verte that same year.

In 2011, following petitions by the Fédération Française des Spiritueux which represents French distillers, the French absinthe ban of 1915 was repealed.

---

[15] *The Dedalus Book of Absinthe, Baker, Phil (2001, p. 165, ISBN 1873982941)*

8.   How It's Made

Distilled Absinthe

Distilled absinthe is made using a base alcohol made from white grapes called *eau de vie*. This translates literally from French as 'water of life', but in French it is a generic term for distilled spirits.

The first stage is called maceration. The botanical ingredients are added to the *eau de vie*: grande wormwood, green anise, and fennel. They are steeped or soaked in the alcohol, which causes them to soften and break down, releasing their complex compounds and flavours.

The spirit is then redistilled one or more times in order to achieve the desired complexity. At this stage it is colourless and leaves the still at around 72% ABV (144 Proof). It can then be diluted (optional) and then bottled as *absinthe blanche* or *la bleue*. For *absinthe verte*, the process moves on to the next stage.

Absinthe verte obtains its unique green colour from the chlorophyll of the botanical ingredients, which are added for secondary maceration. Several other ingredients are also added for complexity of flavour, such as hyssop, melissa, star anise, angelica, peppermint, coriander, veronica, etc.

The chlorophyll remains chemically active, which is critical in the ageing of the absinthe, in much the same way as tannins are in wine.

Distilled absinthe is regarded as the original and superior product. Unlike other spirits and liqueurs, there is a lack of regulation governing its classification, labelling, and base ingredients.

Only Switzerland regulates that absinthe made and sold in Switzerland must be distilled and coloured using natural ingredients.

Cold Mixed Absinthe

The cold mix process evolved along with the geography of where absinthe was made and sold after the ban, and out of the commercial necessity of finding simpler, less expensive, less time-consuming, and more cost effective means of production, making absinthe available to all.

A business person might have asked a number of absinthe drinkers what they find so appealing about absinthe, and they might have heard such replies as: 'the *strength* of it', 'the *colour* of it', 'the bitter *taste*'. Maybe it didn't matter to drinkers what changes were made to production, as long as the product ticked those boxes.

Cold mixed absinthes are often bottled at higher strengths than distilled absinthes, sometimes as much as 90% ABV (180 Proof). They are often brightly coloured using artificial colouring, and flavoured using flavouring essences that are blended in a neutral commercial alcohol base.

Because of a lack of regulation, some producers claim that the base spirit is created by distillation, and therefore it is still a distilled product.

9.   Paraphernalia, Absinthania, and Ritual

Absinthe Spoons

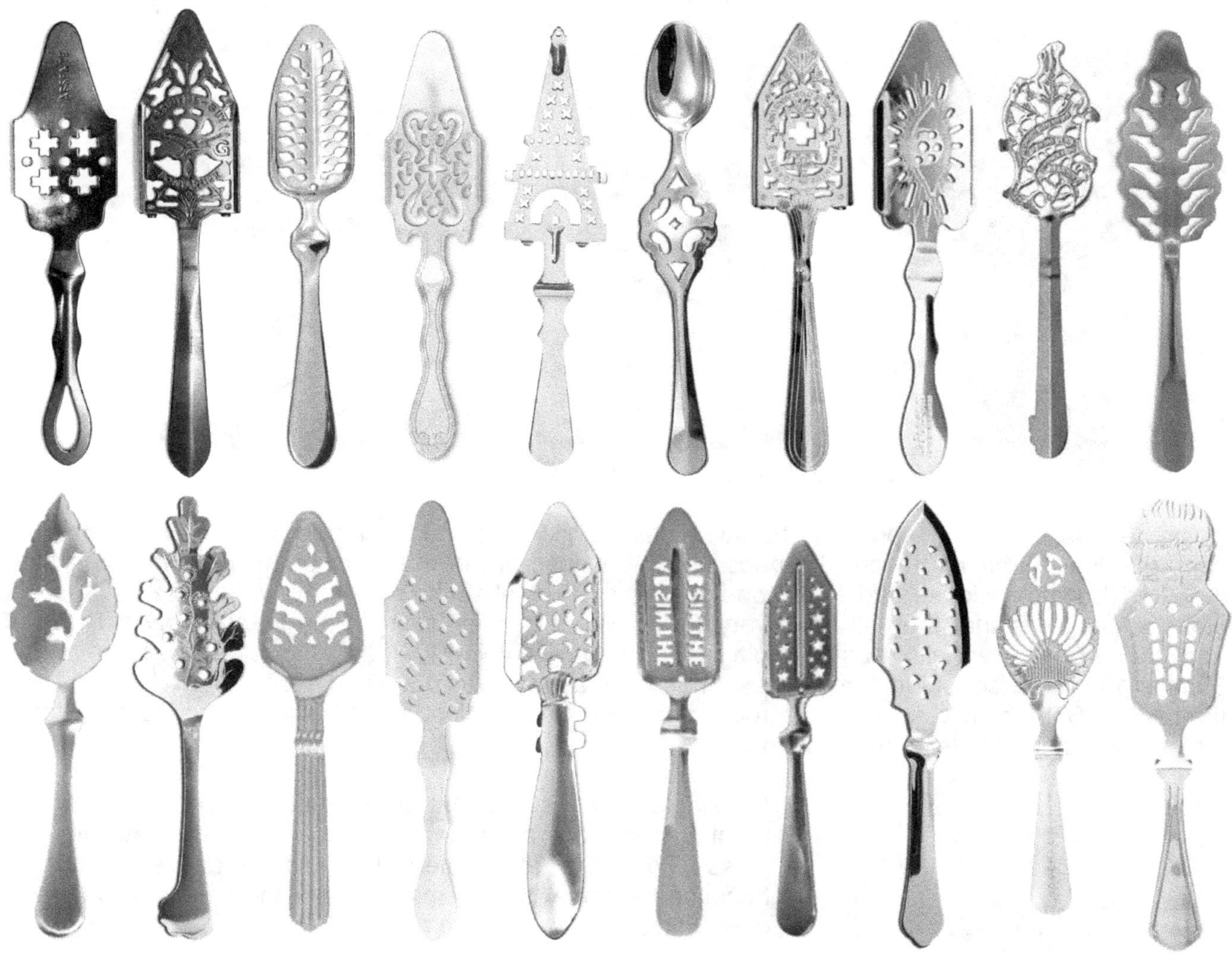

A selection of absinthe spoons (author's collection)

The absinthe spoon helps to break down the sugar cube into the absinthe. It does this by balancing on top of the glass, by means of a small notch which fits on to the rim of the glass, holding it in place while the absinthe is poured over. Absinthe spoons are usually made of stainless steel and are highly polished with a smooth glossy surface, avoiding sharp edges.

While this function is the same for every absinthe spoon, the designs are beautifully varied. Some designs contain references to the wormwood leaf. Some designs refer to places in France such as Pontarlier, or the Eiffel tower, or Switzerland i.e. the Swiss cross. Some spoons are evocative of, and inspired by, Art Nouveau or Art Deco.

Absinthe Glasses

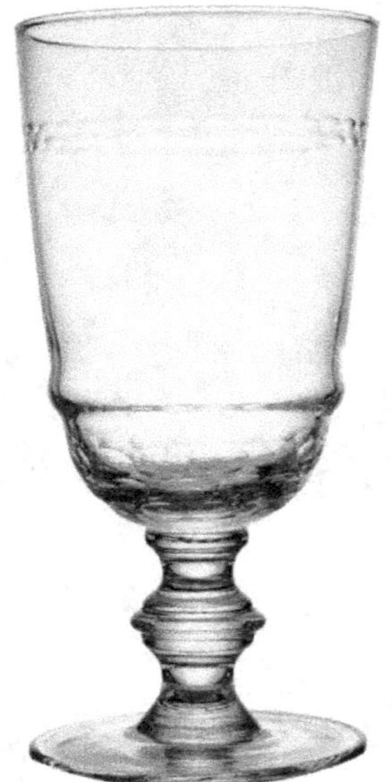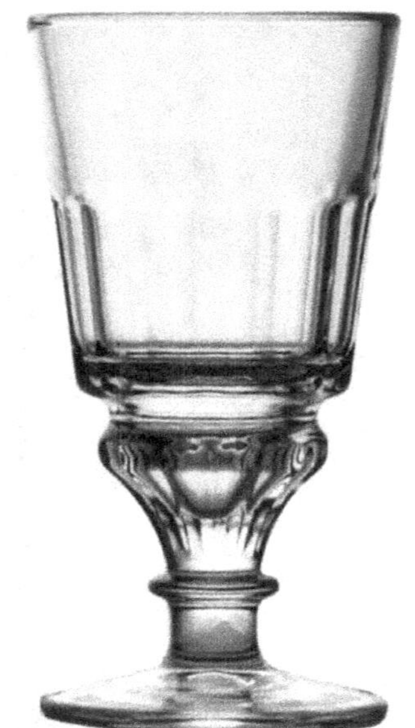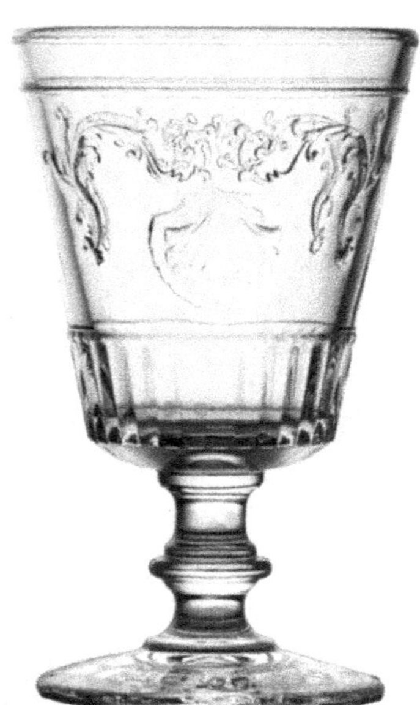

A selection of absinthe glasses (author's collection)

Absinthe glasses initially appear to be stylistically similar to a medieval goblet of the imagination, or even the 'Holy Grail' as it were. Perhaps this is because of the revival of gothic art and architecture that had become widespread in Europe at the time of absinthe's heyday. What makes absinthe glasses unique is that they all have varying indicators at their stem of the ideal or perfect level of absinthe to be poured, either as a simple line, or as a reservoir. The ideal amount is said to be around 30ml or 1 fluid ounce, but in some cases it has been as much as 45ml or 1 ½ fluid ounces. Perhaps in the case of Bohemian absinthe, the larger measures offset against much of the alcohol being burnt off during the flaming stage of preparation.

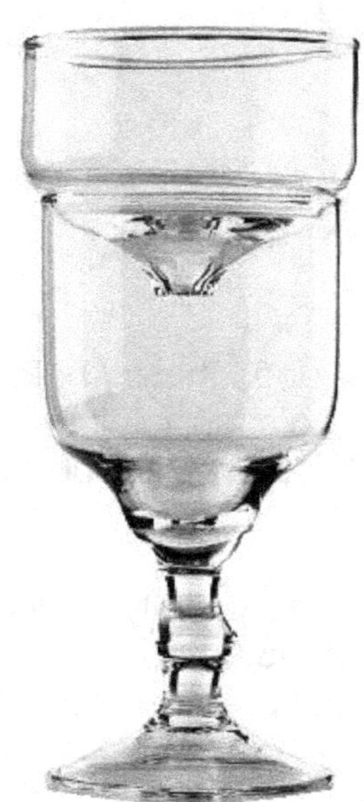

For single servings of absinthe without the need for the use of a fountain there are absinthe drippers, which drip water into the glass. They are also referred to as 'scramblers', perhaps because they offer the absinthe drinker the means to prepare a glass in a hurry.

The simplest of these drippers is a glass dripper which sits neatly on top of the glass (pictured, left).

More complex and elaborate drippers are made of stainless steel in the form of bowls which sit on top of the glass, some of which have small pipes protruding from the bottom of the bowl and into the glass.

More elaborate still are stainless steel drippers with three or more legs which sit high on top of the glass. Underneath the main reservoirs are small funnels which drip onto tiny channels which disperse the droplets into the glass.

An absinthe glass with a dripper
(author's collection)

Absinthe Fountains

The absinthe fountain provides the drips of ice-cold water, which slowly and steadily unlock the complex herbal oils and their flavours kept in solution by the high alcohol content of the absinthe. This process is what turns the absinthe cloudy, and is known as the '*louche*'. As a general rule of thumb, the slower the dripping process, the fuller the flavour. The flavour can also be subtly enhanced by adding mint leaves or cucumber to the water (shown below).

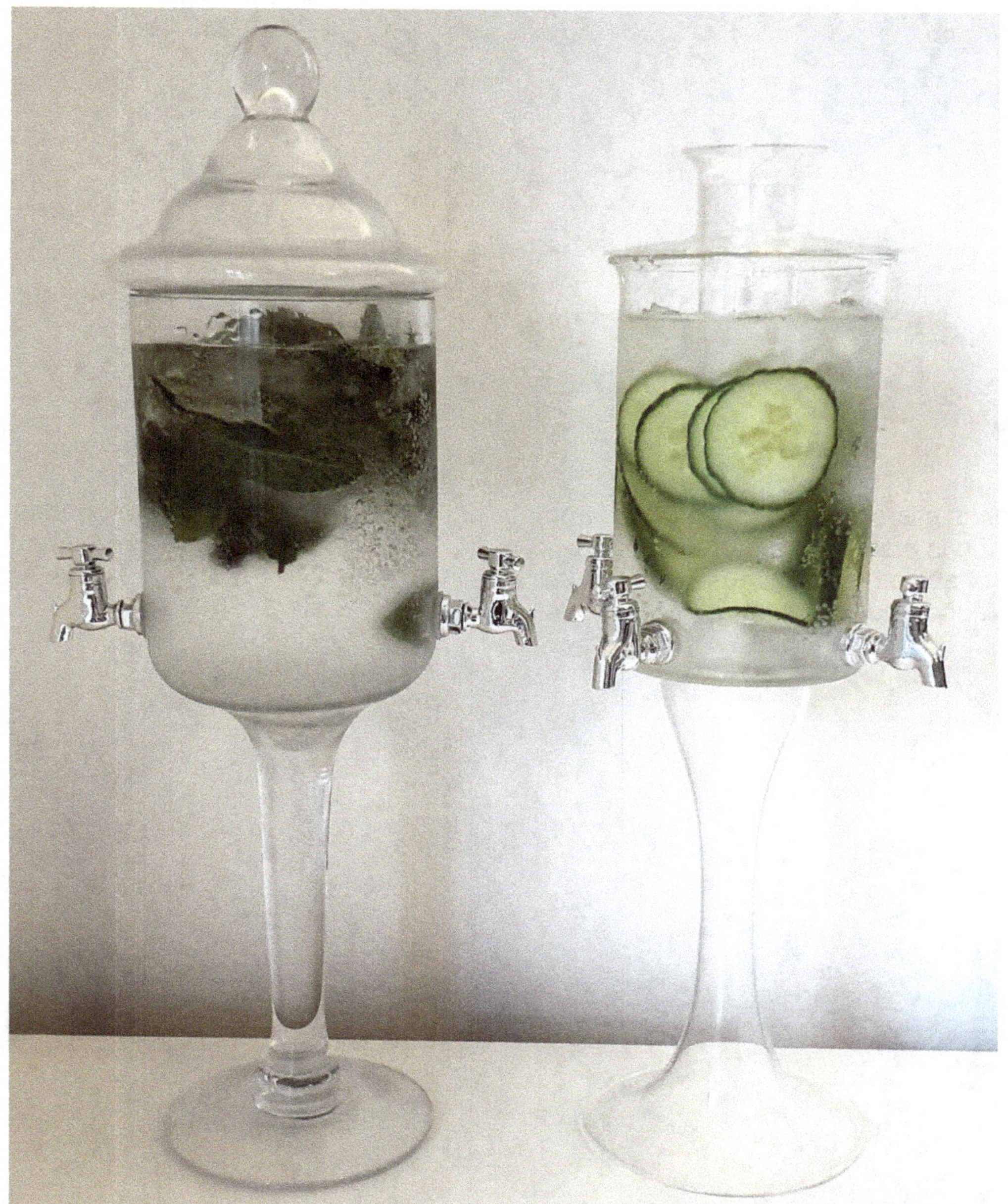

Absinthe fountains (Left: two spout design, Right: four spout design) (author's collection)

From the simplest designs to the most elaborate, there are a large number of different absinthe fountains available, all channelling the look and feel of *La Belle Époque* in their own way. They are made with different combinations of glass and stainless steel or other metals depending on their design, with increasingly elaborately decorated lids and blown glass textures. Before the invention of the absinthe fountain, the dripping process was performed using a carafe of water.

The Traditional Ritual

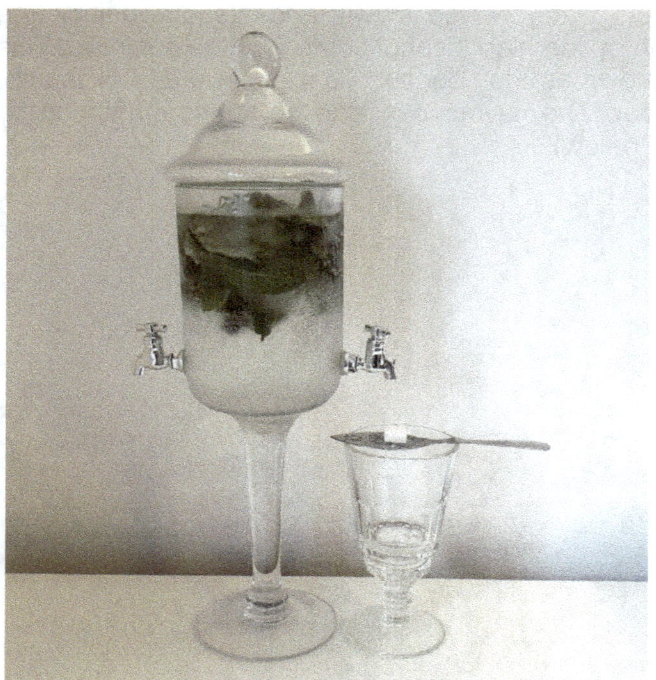

1. The spoon is placed on top of the glass, and a sugar cube is placed on top of the spoon.
A measure of absinthe is poured over the sugar cube and into the glass.

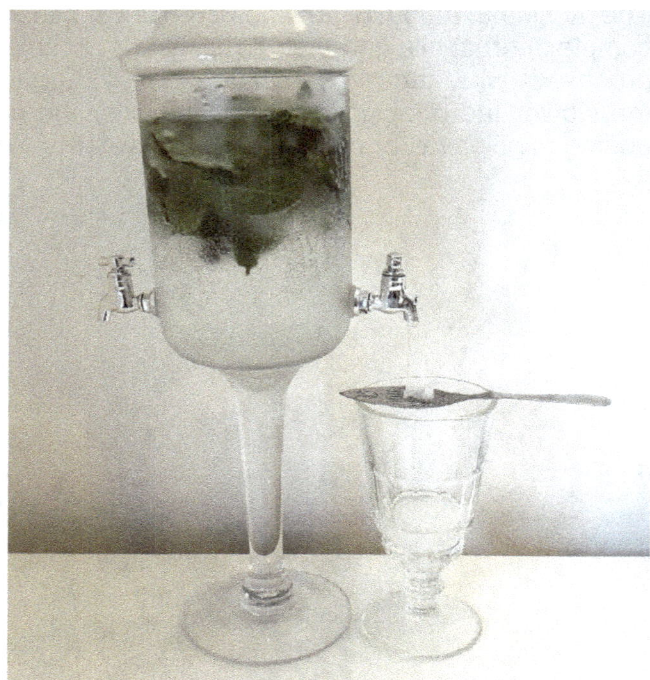

2. Ice-cold water is slowly dripped onto the sugar cube so that it breaks down into the glass.

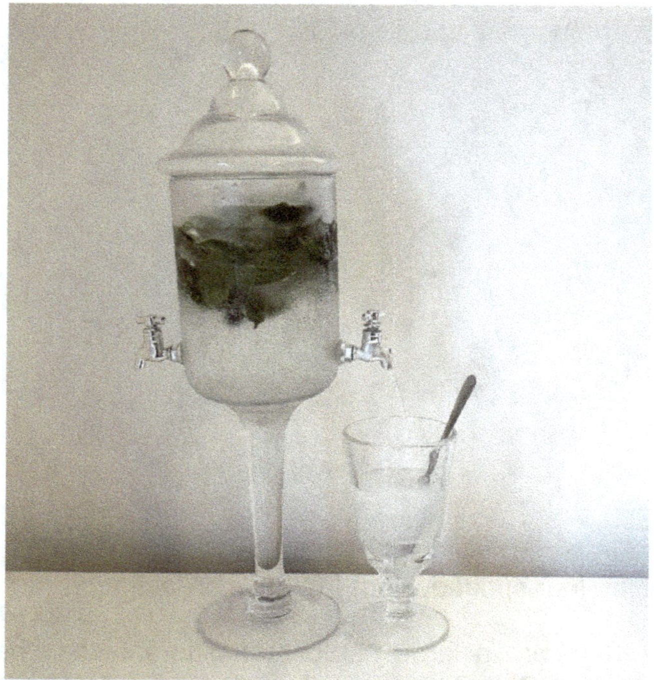

3. The water is added at a ratio of 3 to 5 parts water to 1 part absinthe.

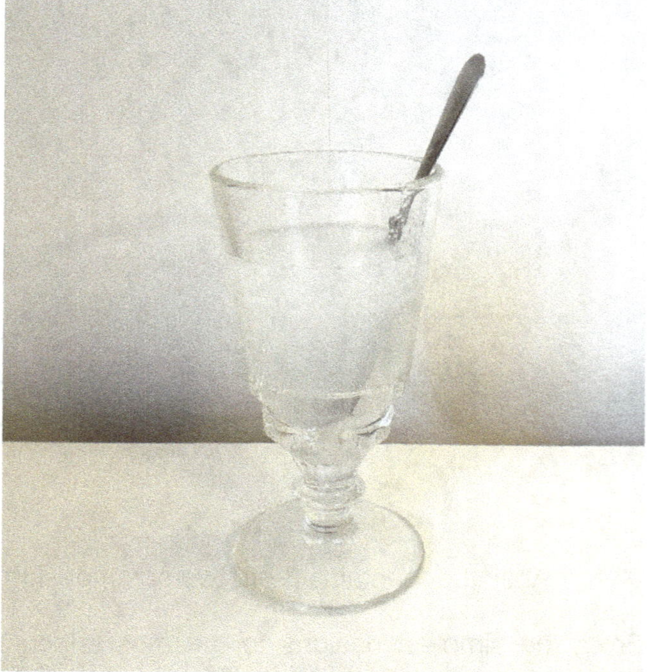

4. Stirred and enjoyed.

The Bohemian Ritual.

In the modern world, unlike the 19th century, it is necessary to say the following: The description below is included for interest only and is by no means instructional. Any use of a flame should only be undertaken by a competent person, with great care and attention, and with the appropriate safety measures in place.

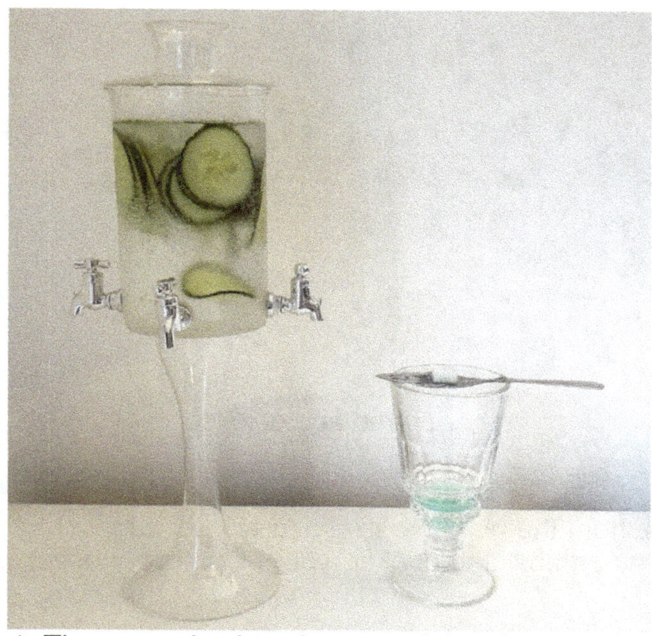

1. The spoon is placed on top of the glass, and a sugar cube is placed on top of the spoon.
A measure of absinthe is poured over the sugar cube and into the glass.

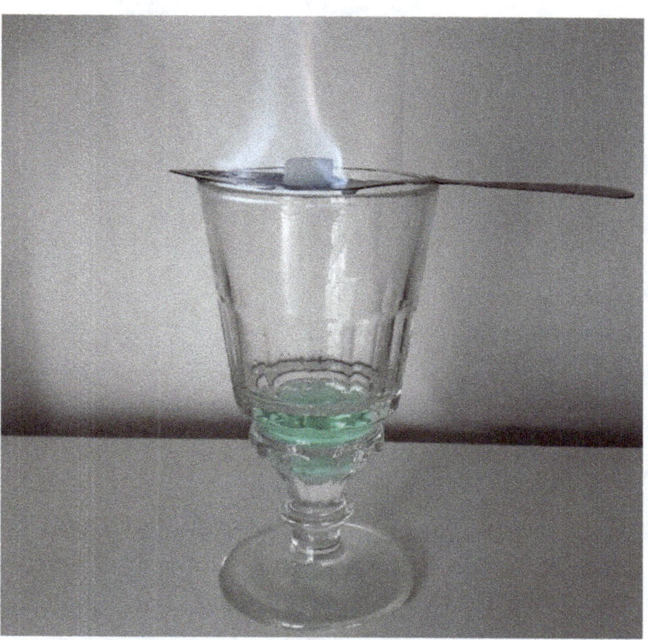

2. The sugar is set alight so that it bubbles and caramelises.

Note: The time it takes for the sugar to bubble and caramelise varies depending on the density of the sugar cube and the alcohol content of the absinthe.

The spoon is not to be left resting on the glass for too long, as the heat of the flame conducted through the spoon may cause the glass to shatter.

The spoon is held above the glass either periodically or throughout.

Glasses are not moved or carried while any flame is lit.

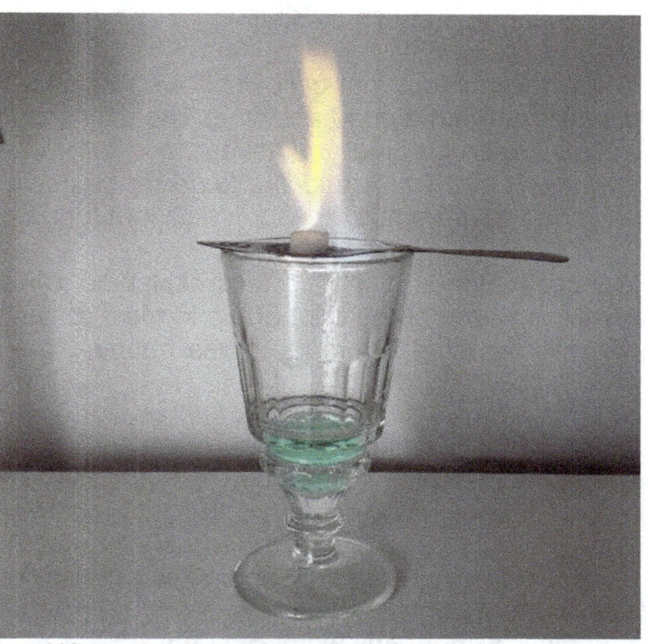

3. When the flame has died down, the sugar is stirred into the absinthe.

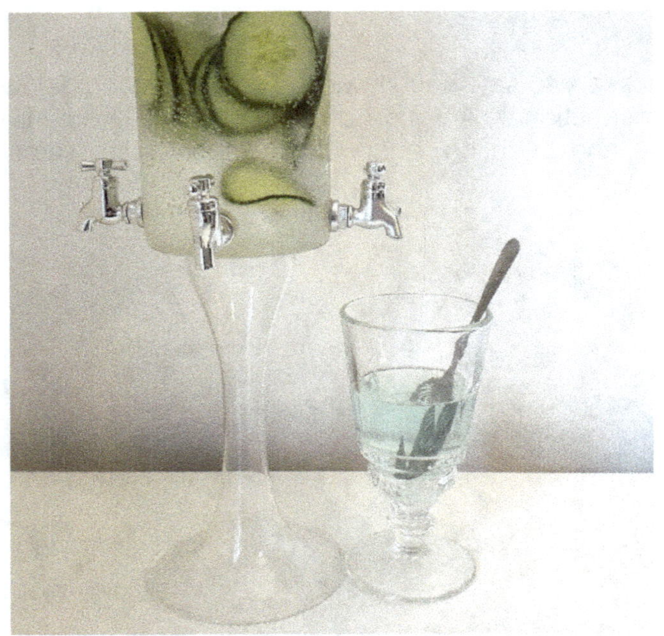

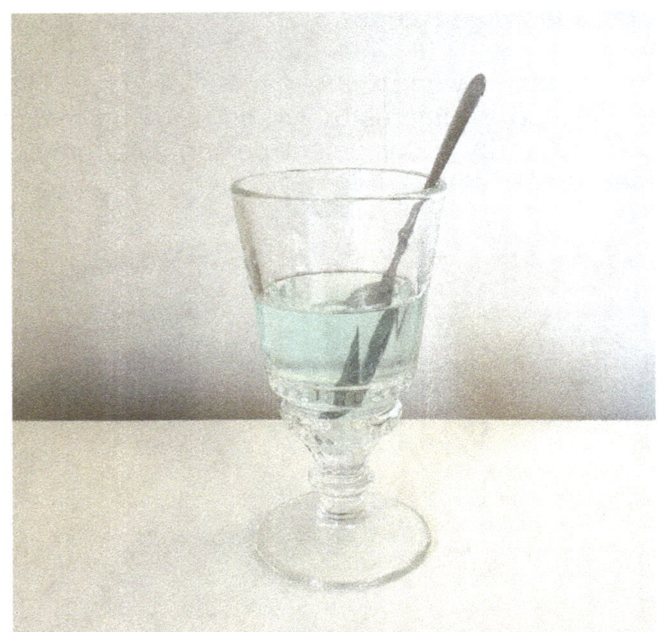

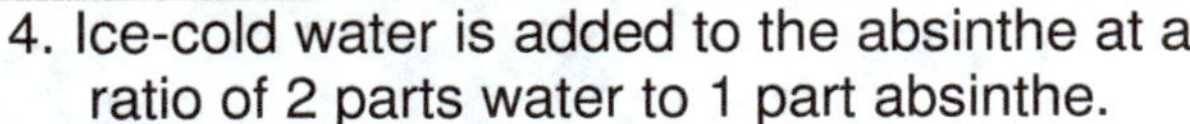

4. Ice-cold water is added to the absinthe at a ratio of 2 parts water to 1 part absinthe.

5. Stirred and enjoyed.

There are of course many variations to these rituals, from the number, size, and type of sugar cubes used, to how much water to absinthe ratio is used. As an absinthe drinker, you will probably develop your own variation to suite your taste.

Going out for an Absinthe

Over the last couple of decades since the lifting of the ban and the reintroduction of absinthe, a number of drinking establishments have emerged to cater for those wishing to try absinthe, either on its own, or as part of a cocktail.

Any establishment that calls itself an 'Absinthe Bar' should have the necessary facilities available to provide you with a good absinthe. The staff should be knowledgeable and able to recommend different brands based on type and flavour, and talk you through the ways in which they offer to serve it, and how much of it you would like to do for yourself, i.e. pouring the desired amount of water, etc. If they have one or more absinthe fountains mounted on top of the bar, you should be in for a treat.

In a bar in Soho, London, I once explained to a Danish bartender how to prepare an absinthe using a carafe of water for the drip. She told me that she was not familiar with absinthe and she believed that it was still illegal in Denmark. I was happy, I got my drink, and it all added to the fun of the positive experience.

While many bars are friendly and accommodating, unfortunately there are still some that have a variety of restrictions in place. Perhaps this is because of too many previous bad outcomes from groups of people downing absinthe shots and becoming unruly, out of control, or even violently ill.

Such incidents are sadly responsible for the notoriety that absinthe still has. This is also due to the lack of knowledge on how to serve and drink it correctly, and the bars who still offer to serve it in a shot glass without any water or sugar.

In a bar in the Googe Street area of London I asked for an absinthe, and it was served in a shot glass. I asked for a couple of sugar cubes and a glass of water with ice, since I didn't mind preparing it myself. Sometime later when I ordered a second, I was told that they could not serve me another.

I thought to myself that maybe they had imposed a rule of one absinthe per person per night. Disappointed, but willing to accept this rule, I asked if I could instead have a pastis or some other anise spirit or liqueur, which I would then water down in the same way (The New Orleans style Sazerac cocktail sometimes contains pastis or other anise flavoured liqueurs as a substitute if absinthe is not available). But no. I was told that because they had served me just one absinthe, they were not allowed to serve me anything else at all... AT ALL.

In a bar in the Shoreditch area of London, I asked the bartender for an absinthe, and he told me that he was not allowed to serve it to me on its own, only in cocktails. I said that I didn't want it on its own, I wanted a glass of ice cold water poured onto it, and that I didn't mind if he did it, or if I did it myself. He was under the impression that this was illegal and refused to serve me.

In a bar in the Liverpool Street area of London, I noticed a Pernod absinthe bottle among those on display. I asked for a glass of Pernod absinthe, but when it was being poured I was surprised to see that the colour was nothing like the deep herbal green of Pernod absinthe. It was a bright turquoise in colour. It dawned on me that the contents of the bottle had been replaced with a bohemian absinthe and passed off as Pernod...

...Maybe their thinking was: 'all absinthes are the same', or they replaced it with something with less alcohol content thinking: 'the bottle looks good, and as long as people get drunk on the shots, it doesn't matter what absinthe it is, they're too stupid to know the difference anyway'.

Perhaps some of this is due to the English and their relationship with alcohol. In England for example, absinthe can be purchased from a few specialist shops. In France however (and certainly other countries in Europe as well), most supermarkets will have part of their alcohol section dedicated to absinthe and pastis, in quantities ranging from 35cl to 1.5l bottles. Perhaps this is because of the well established tradition of the aperitif or aperitivo, particularly in Mediterranean countries.

Making your own absinthe

The revival of interest in absinthe has led to a number of absinthe making kits, offering customers the opportunity to attempt to make their own homemade absinthe. They often use vodka as the alcohol base, and involve soaking herbs, oils, or extracts.

In the hands of the customer, using the wrong amount of herbs, oils, or extracts to make the mixture 'stronger' or 'tastier' can be dangerous and potentially poisonous.

While the result can be quite different from the genuine article, these kits do offer a fun and interesting hands-on experience and insight into how alcoholic beverages are made using the cold mix method

To Your Health

Because of the Swiss-French history of Absinthe, a common toast when drinking in company is '*santé!*' (literally 'health' or 'to good health').

In this spirit, the reader is advised to please drink responsibly, well, and in style.

10.　　Notable References in Popular Culture

Absinthe in the past

- Part of the iconography and the zeitgeist of the period depicted.
- An illicit mysterious vice.

1992	Film	**Bram Stoker's Dracula** Dracula (Gary Oldman) serves Mina (Winona Ryder) a glass of absinthe while seducing her: *"Absinthe is the aphrodisiac of the self. The Green Fairy who lives in the absinthe wants your soul. But you are safe with me".*
2001	Film	**From Hell** Investigating the murders of Jack the Ripper, Frederick Abberline (Johnny Depp), grieving the loss of his wife who died during childbirth, drinks absinthe laced with laudanum to numb his pain.
2002	Film	**Moulin Rouge** Paris, 1900, La Belle Époque, characters experience hallucinations after drinking absinthe. The Green Fairy is portrayed by Kylie Minogue.
2003	Book	**The Second Glass of Absinthe** by Michelle Black An absinthe hallucination may or may not have inspired a murder in 1880, Leadville, Colorado.
2003	TV Series	**Carnivàle** (HBO) Set in the 1930s during the Great Depression, absinthe is frequently consumed by the mysterious blind seer Professor Lodz (Patrick Bauchau).
2004	Film	**Van Helsing** Gabriel Van Helsing (Hugh Jackman) explains to Anna Valerious (Kate Beckinsale) that his curiosity is what keeps him going. He then opens a half-bottle of bohemian style absinthe, which Anna takes and toasts him, saying "Here's to what keeps you going". Van Helsing advises her "Absinthe, strong stuff".
2012	Book	**The Absinthe Cloud** (Le Page & Dupuy #1) by Timothy Everhart Paris, 1900, La Belle Époque, French Intelligence agents Robert LePage and Patrick Dupuy attempt to stop an anarchist plot to bomb the city.

Absinthe in the present

- An illicit mysterious vice.
- A remnant of a bygone age, a dark past.

1999	Book	**The Basic Eight** by Daniel Handler Absinthe figures heavily in the plot of the book, which features Bohemian characters who are drawn to absinthe by its 'dangerous history'.
2004	TV Series	**The Thirsty Traveller** (Grasslands Entertainment / Fine Living Channel) In series 3 Episode 7 titled "The Green Fairy", the host travels to several distilleries in different countries and observes the process and flavours of contemporary absinthe.

Aside from the above, there are a number of references to absinthe in popular culture which play on rumour and mythology to engage the imagination of the audience. The myth about it being hallucinogenic is frequently used as a precursor to a 'hallucination sequence' or 'dream sequence', where 'visions' are revealed, a person behaves out of character, or a person's true character emerges.

A typical conversation on the subject of absinthe:

Me: Have you tried absinthe?

Other: Yeah, it was awful, eugh!

Me: Did you have it in the traditional way with the water and the sugar?

Other: What?